THE ART OF
JAPANESE
PRINTS

THE ART OF
JAPANESE
PRINTS

RICHARD ILLING

OCTOPUS

ISBN 0 7064 1380 6

First American Edition

Printed in Hong Kong by Mandarin Offset International Limited

Note on print sizes
Japanese prints normally come in standard sizes. In the captions these are referred to by name. The approximate sizes are:

Aiban: 13½ × 8¾ in (34 × 22 cm)
Bai-oban: 18 × 13½ in (46 × 34 cm)
Chuban: 10¼ × 7½ in (26 × 19 cm)
Chu-tanzaku: 15 × 5 in (38 × 13 cm)
Hashira-e: 27½ – 29½ × 4¾ – 6 in (70–75 × 12–15 cm)
Hosoban: 13 × 5¾ in (33 × 14.5 cm)
Kakemono-e: 29½ × 10 in (75 × 25 cm)
Koban: 9 × 6¾ in (23 × 17 cm)
Naga-ban: 19¾ × 9 in (50 × 23 cm)
Oban: 15 × 10 in (38 × 25 cm)
O-tanzaku: 15 × 6¾ in (38 × 17 cm)
Shikishiban: 8¼ × 7 in (21 × 18 cm)

1. (*Frontispiece*) Kiyonaga, *Viewing the cherry blossom at Asukayama*, late 1780s. *Oban* colour print, right-hand sheet of a triptych. London, British Museum.

Contents

1
Introduction

Japanese wood-block prints are the most popular form of Far Eastern art to reach the Western world. This is hardly surprising since the prints were a highly developed art form, expressly intended to give pleasure to ordinary men and women. They were designed by accomplished artists, printed by unsurpassed techniques and, when first seen in the West, presented a complete contrast with previous artistic traditions. They remain a source of inspiration that no artist or designer can afford to ignore. At the same time these prints open a window on many aspects of the beautiful and fascinating world of feudal Japan.

Their more general popularity is aided by their availability. The fact that they tended to be underrated yet plentiful in Japan in the late nineteenth and early twentieth centuries allowed their wholesale shipment to the dealers and auction houses in the West. Many are available for study in public collections in Europe and the U.S.A. and others have found their way back to Japan. It is still, however, as easy to find Japanese prints for sale in London, Paris or New York as in Tokyo and they remain cheap enough for the amateur collector to envisage owning original examples.

The prints were produced entirely by hand, without recourse to printing presses, by a team of craftsmen employed and overseen by a publisher. The publisher, whether he was commissioned to provide a print for private circulation or, more usually, simply as a personal commercial venture, was the linchpin of the system that brought together the necessary skills. He owned the workshops, where the craftsmen made the prints, and the sales outlets, which were often the same premises (plates 3, 4). The artist, usually an independent contractor working from his own studio, would provide an initial sketch for a design ordered by the publisher. This would be drawn in black ink on white paper to the correct dimensions for the wood-block (plate 7). This brush drawing would go to the publisher, who employed a skilled copyist to trace the original design onto thin paper, fining down the lines for the engraver. A specialist calligrapher was sometimes employed for important textual matter on a print. The finished copy was passed to the engraver, who pasted it face down on to a block of seasoned cherry wood, planed along the grain. The blocks were made in standard sizes to fit the usual paper sizes (see the Glossary). When partly dry, the back of the paper was rubbed away gently with the

2. Kunisada II, *The actor Ichikawa Danjuro VII*, 1852. *Oban* colour print. Private Collection.
From a fine set of prints supposedly illustrating scenes from Bakin's novel *Hakkenden* (see p. 120). The actor is not named but his facial features are unmistakable and would have been easily recognized by his fans. This powerful design shows how good an artist Kunisada II could be.

3. Settan (1778–1843), *The Publisher's shop, Tsuruya*. Double page book illustration from *Famous Views of Edo*, 1833. 8½ × 12½ in (21.3 × 31.5 cm). Private Collection.
A fascinating view of the busy street with the open print shop.

fingers until the lines could be clearly seen. Hemp seed oil was applied to make the remaining paper more transparent. The block was then carved, using a variety of chisels and fine cutting tools, to leave the design standing out in relief in reversed image.

The registration of the colours, was achieved by the *kento*, a right-angled ridge at the lower right-hand corner and a short straight ridge on the left side. These were left in relief on the original block, the keyblock. The lines of the keyblock were inked and a number of proofs were pulled, one for each colour required. These were, in their turn, laid on to fresh blocks and the areas for each colour were engraved. The finished blocks would be washed carefully to remove the last traces of adherent paper and, when they were dry, the printer would set to work. Kneeling or sitting in front of the block, surrounded by his brushes and dishes of inks, dyes and pigments, he would take a sheet of paper that had been moistened and left in a press for some hours to allow it to absorb and take the ink well. The ink or colour was applied to the block, the paper aligned with the ridges of the *kento* and laid on the block. The impression was taken by rubbing the back of the paper with a *baren*. The *baren* was an oiled pad of bamboo-leaf fibre wrapped round a circular card. A separate printing from each of the colour blocks in turn was required to produce a colour print. Gradation of colour was achieved by carefully wiping away some of the ink on the block before printing. Various special effects using gums, lacquers, mica, metal dusts or mother of pearl required the burnishing of the print after

4. Eishi, *Print Sellers shop*, late 1780s.
Chuban colour print. Tokyo National
Museum.

it had been made. Blind printed, or embossed, patterns called for greater pressure than could be applied with the *baren* and, traditionally, a polished boar's tusk was used.

The finished print was hung up to dry and then trimmed and put out for sale. It seems that an edition would normally run to about two hundred copies. The wood-blocks were framed to prevent warping and stored, to be reused if further editions were called for. The pigments were vegetable extracts, minerals or, later, imported chemical dyes. Red lead, red ochre, indigo, orpiment, gamboge and rouge were used either alone or mixed together or with the extracts from barks or roots. Ultramarine was introduced in the 1820s. Aniline dyes are first found in prints of 1864 and were used extensively in the late 1870s and 1880s. Vegetable dyes were usually applied mixed with a little rice paste. Various black inks were used, mostly derived from pine-soot or lamp-black, mixed with resins, glue or alum to give different effects. White lead, powdered kaolin or finely ground clam shells mixed with glue gave white colours. Special effects included mica flakes sprinkled onto a mixture of rice paste and alum. Powdered metallic brass and copper were used on especially luxurious prints such as *surimono* to give a silver or coppery sheen to parts of the design.

There were many subjects but, for the popular broadsheets at least, the *kabuki* theatre and the courtesans of the licensed brothel quarters provided the bulk of the material.

Kabuki, like many popular arts, had diverse roots. It seemed to thrive

6. (*Right*) Hiroshige and Toyokuni III (Kunisada),
*The Lady Fujitsubo watching Prince Genji departing in
the moonlight*, Chapter 13, *Akashi*, from *Fashionable
Genji*, 1853. *Oban* colour-printed triptych. Private
Collection.
One of the best of a celebrated series of collaborative
triptychs by Hiroshige and Kunisada. Kunisada drew
the figures of Fujitsubo and her attendant, Hiroshige
designed the moonlit landscape.

5. (*Left*) Kunisada, *The pledge of loyalty in the Peach-orchard*, c.1830. *Oban* colour-printed triptych. Private Collection.
Three famous Chinese heroes, Kuan Yü (right), Liu Pei (middle) and Chang Fei (left) who met together in the latter's peach orchard in AD 184 and made a pact of brotherhood in defence of the house of Han. They were admired in Japan for their steadfast loyalty to each other in spite of many trials. Chang Fei later became Emperor of Wu at the time of the Three Kingdoms.

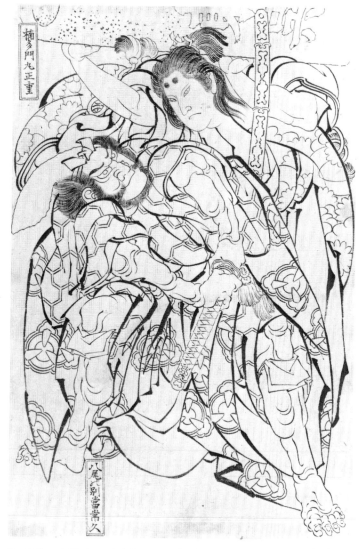

7. (*Above*) Hokusai, *The young hero Kusunoki Masashige attacking Yao Tsunehisa*, c.1830. Original preparatory drawing ink on paper, 15 × 10¾ in (38 × 27 cm). Private Collection.

8. (*Above right*) Hokusai, *The young hero Kusunoki Masashige Tsunehisa*, c.1830. *Oban* colour print. Courtesy Sotheby Parke Bernet & Co.
Comparing this print with the drawing in plate 7, it is interesting to see how much of the details of the patterns were left to the publisher's team to complete.

on restrictions and adversity, which prevented complacency and stagnation. It began in the early seventeenth century as impromptu performances by bawdy temple dancing girls who were suppressed for immorality. These were succeeded by troupes of young male dancers, who were in turn suppressed for different immorality. These gave way eventually to professional male entertainers who took both male and female roles. To accentuate their maturity they had to shave their forelocks and when acting female parts they covered the bare foreheads with a patch of cloth (plate 40).

The ability to dance remained central to an actor's technique. An orchestra provided the music, skilled chanters sang out the dialogue, allowing the actors scope to develop movement, posture and dancing to express the emotions and tensions demanded by the plot.

The government continued to disapprove of *kabuki* as popular entertainment and *samurai* were forbidden to attend. The theatres were restricted to certain areas but this only served to crystallize their appeal for the rest of the townsfolk and produced a specialized *kabuki* world with its own well-loved and popular traditions.

The actors organized themselves into 'families'. Training began in childhood although occasionally talented newcomers might join a family by adoption. In each family the names of famous predecessors became labels for various levels of attainment and an actor might graduate to the name of a more illustrious forebear as he became more skilled and mature. In due course he might relinquish his name to an up-and-coming junior as he advanced further up the grades. There was always pressure on an actor to live up to the reputation of his name and, if possible, to add fresh lustre to it.

The theatres themselves were constructed from wood and had no artificial lighting for fear of fire. The lanterns shown in plate 12 were ornamental and served to advertise the *mon* (crests) of the actors. The stage projected into the auditorium and had an extension running through the audience along which the actors could make particularly spectacular entrances and exits. With the passage of time the stage itself became an increasingly ingenious structure with multiple revolving sections and trap doors which allowed actors to appear and disappear suddenly.

There were six theatrical seasons each year, each lasting as long as it was supported by public response. Performances would last all day with intervals between plays. The plays were broadly categorized into *jidaimono*, based on famous historical episodes, and *sewamono*, plays about everyday contemporary life. There were various sub-divisions and, in addition, performances which were entirely displays of dancing with no plots.

The popular prints had close links with the *kabuki* and several of the most admired artists worked almost exclusively at actor prints. It is likely that many of the prints were commissioned or subsidized by the actors or theatre managers for advertisement. Most often we are shown the actor during a performance, caught at a critical moment of the play. Such poses usually involved a curious dramatic technique, the *mie*. This was a transient, melodramatic, fixed pose with a special facial expression. At the climax of a scene of particular emotional tension the actor drew himself up, arms often outstretched, the body rigid. His head was moved several times with a circular motion until, at the crescendo of the *mie*, his eyes dilated and seemed almost to bulge from their sockets, while the pupils slowly turned inwards. This odd squinting appearance, difficult to achieve effectively but much appreciated by the audience, explains some of the extraordinary, grimacing faces of many of the actor prints. This was sometimes accentuated by their make-up (plate 43).

With diligence, luck, the ability to read a certain amount of Japanese, and appropriate reference books, it is often possible to identify the role of the actor and the name of the play. If one is fortunate, these will lead to the story which enormously enhances the interest of the prints, as seemingly irrelevant details of the picture take on added meaning.

The licenced entertainment and brothel quarters, of which the *Yoshiwara* in Edo is the best known example, was a further important source of material for the popular prints. Edo in the seventeenth

9. Utamaro, *Lovers on a balcony*,
1788. *Oban* colour-printed album plate
from *The Poem of the Pillow*.
London, British Museum.
One of Utamaro's finest designs
from his earliest and best album of
erotica.

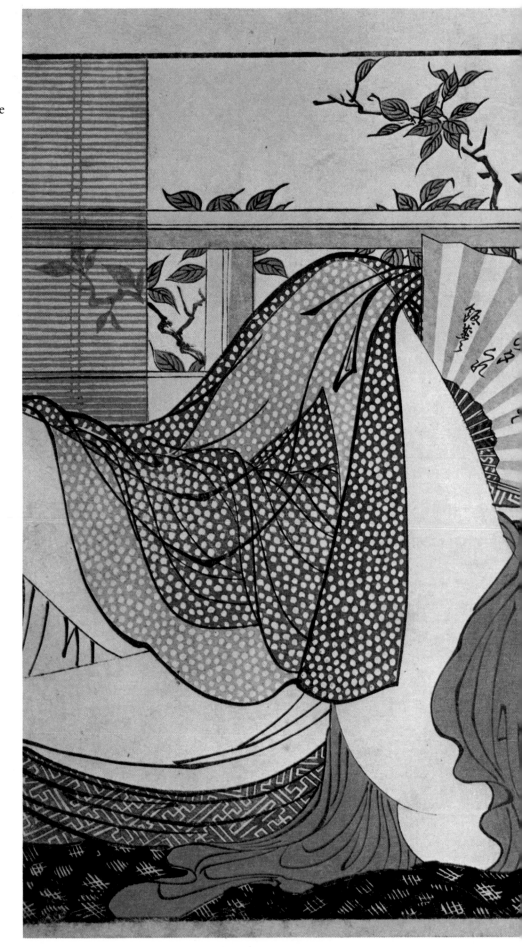

10. Hiroshige, *Cat on Windowsill, The Festival of the Cock, Asakusa Ricefields*, from *One Hundred Views of Edo*, 1857. *Oban* colour print. Private Collection. These two impressions have been chosen to demonstrate the changes that tend to occur with later reprintings. The early impression (left) shows a crisply printed, unbroken, sharp keyblock with carefully applied and gradated colour (note especially the thatched roof, Mount Fuji, the haunch of the cat and the decorated cartouche of the subtitle). The later impression, using fewer, cheaper, more garish pigments, shows faults in colour registration and evidence of worn blocks.

11. Kuniyoshi, *Imperial Wardens sitting by their watch-fire*, illustrating a poem by Yoshinobu, from *One Hundred poems by one hundred poets*, c.1840. *Oban* colour print. Private Collection.
With many of the prints from this set quite marked differences in the colouring occur. The impression with the grey background is probably slightly earlier and uses an extra block for more trees in the background. In this instance however, the colour variations are not, in themselves, indicative of a late reprinting but seem to represent experimentation by the publisher and his printer to obtain different effects.

century has been described as a 'city of bachelors' and the authorities not only condoned prostitution but attempted to regulate it. The original *Yoshiwara* was opened in 1618, modelled on the established licenced quarters of the *Shimabara* in Kyoto and the *Shimmachi* in Osaka. In 1657, after a great fire had destroyed much of Edo, the 'new' *Yoshiwara* was established on the north-eastern outskirts of the city. In this segregated, walled enclave, entered through a single, guarded gate, a long, broad central thoroughfare, planted with flowering cherry trees, ran its length with side-streets up to half a mile long. There were over a hundred brothels, about four hundred tea-houses, and shrines and the living quarters of not only the several thousand prostitutes but all the attendants, entertainers and others who lived in this enclosed town within a town.

The brothels were classified into grades and, within them, the girls were each stratified according to their beauty, experience and other accomplishments. All these factors would, of course, be reflected in their price. The highest grades of prostitute had a degree of choice about whom they entertained and they expected to be courted by their admirers with love letters and appropriate gifts. These girls are usually referred to as courtesans. Only the most wealthy could patronize them but their presence, by setting the highest standards of elegance, refinement and sexual accomplishment, influenced the quality of the lower grades of prostitutes, who strove to emulate them.

The *Yoshiwara* was more than just an outlet for the sexually deprived Edo manhood. Within its walls the distinctions of the otherwise rigid class system were diminished, and the lower-caste but wealthy merchant's son could cut a fine figure in these more relaxed and frivolous surroundings. As dusk fell and the lanterns were lit, music, songs and dancing began. *Samurai* would rub shoulders with townsmen and, in the tea-houses, the other creative elements of Japanese society, the poets, authors, artists and thinkers could be found chatting and mingling with the pleasure seekers.

In addition to the courtesan prints there is a quite separate genre of explicit sexual pictures. The Japanese call these erotica *shunga*, 'spring pictures'. They were produced in large numbers by most of the notable designers of the prints. The Japanese were not prudish about sex and, although adultery (being a form of disloyalty) was regarded as a crime, anything that was designed to enhance sexual pleasure found a ready market. Among these can be found some of the most beautiful evocations of passionate love that the world has ever seen. The majority, however, are merely erotic pictures without any special artistic merit. These prints are illustrated by a couple of the most innocuous examples (plates 9, 16). This is by no means indicative of the importance of such works in the development of Japanese prints and readers who are interested to study this aspect of the art will find in the bibliography several excellent, currently available books on the subject.

17

18

A term often encountered in relation to the popular prints of the Edo period (1615–1868) is *ukiyo-e*, usually translated as 'pictures of the floating world'. *Ukiyo* was a medieval Buddhist concept denoting the transience of life in this 'world of suffering'. By the mid-seventeenth century the meaning had altered and the transience of life was seen as an excuse for enjoying frivolous, extravagant, pleasurable pastimes. In the Genroku period (1688–1704) *ukiyo* had come to be used as a prefixed epithet for anything that was new, trendily fashionable, and, above all, tinged with eroticism. It was at about this time that the first commercial printed broadsheets achieved widespread popularity and these, and the paintings in the same style, became known as *ukiyo-e*. The name stuck and has come to be applied to almost all the prints and paintings of the artists working for the plebeian market. This is unfortunate since it has led to the misplaced notion of an *ukiyo-e* 'school' of art where none really existed. These artists, on the contrary, strove to break new ground and constantly changed their styles, rather than trying to follow a canon of artistic norms. Definitions of *ukiyo-e* tend to be vague and rely first on the popular, everyday subject-matter of the pictures and secondly on their deviation from the styles of the Japanese academic schools of painting. This lack of an exact definition of the term has led art historians, who are usually fairly consistent about the beginnings of *ukiyo-e*, into varying opinions about how and when it ended. Typically this had led to argument about whether certain works of artists such as Hokusai and Hiroshige should be classified as *ukiyo-e* or not – a fruitless and artificial exercise.

It is also interesting to review the variations in views regarding the decadence and decline of printmaking in Japan. Early critics extolled the perfection of womanhood portrayed in the 1780s by Kiyonaga and felt that Utamaro's sensual pictures of a decade later were already becoming degenerate and immoral and the art decadent. Later writers accepted that the prints of Utamaro's time were superb but that after his death in 1806 a decline set in, the landscape prints of Hokusai and Hiroshige always excepted. Readers of the older books may find it difficult to understand how so many of the 'decadent' prints of the nineteenth century have come to be so widely admired. As usual such judgements about the decadence of others, often on moral grounds, tend to tell us more about the authors than about their subjects.

Collectors and other enthusiasts have never, of course, paid too much attention to the art critic in such matters and have always continued to patronize what they liked best. It is probably much nearer to the truth to say that every decade from about 1660 until the present day has seen the production of fine Japanese prints even though in some decades these form only a small proportion of the total output.

It is hoped that this book will show something of the wide variety of style and subject which is available for our delight and may lead the reader towards more detailed study of those prints which appeal to him.

12. Okumura Masanobu, *Interior of a Kabuki Theatre*, 1740. Hand-coloured *tan-e*. 18¼ × 26¾ in (46.3 × 67.9 cm). Chicago, Art Institute of Chicago.
A spectacular interior *uki-e* perspective print. The actor Ichikawa Ebizo, in the role of Goro, one of the Soga brothers, is shown in a famous scene, sharpening a huge arrow. He is acting in a small, enclosed, box-like structure on the stage, which serves to concentrate attention on him. Behind him are chanters and a small orchestra. There is a walkway running from the stage through the auditorium. The large open windows high on either side provide the only light.

13. Koryusai, *Early Evening in the Yoshiwara*, c.1776. *Oban* colour print from the album *Twelve Bouts of Passionate Love*. Private Collection.
The man in the centre is about to replenish the young girl's cup with warm *sake*. The frontispiece to an otherwise very erotic set of prints.

14. (*Above*) Buncho, *Lovers listening to the nightingale,* early 1770s. *Chuban* colour print. Private Collection.

15. (*Left*) Koryusai, *Lovers under mosquito net,* c.1770. *Chuban* colour print. Private Collection.

16. (*Right*) Kiyomasu,
*Actors in the roles of Soga no
Goro and Asahina Saburo*,
mid–1710s. *Kakemono-e*,
hand–coloured *tane-e*.
(c.f. plate 129).
London, British Museum.

2
The Early Prints

It took nearly a hundred years for the Japanese print to evolve from the wood-block illustrated books and albums of the seventeenth century to the sophisticated, multi-coloured sheets that form the bulk of the prints that we know to-day. Although the early work is often called 'primitive', this is inaccurate in art-historical terms, since the designs were drawn by professional artists and printed by technically competent, trained craftsmen. The resulting prints, moreover, frequently include some of the acknowledged masterpieces of the art. They are, however, really very rare. The most enthusiastic collectors of the past had difficulty in obtaining more than a handful of good examples and even lesser works from this era are hard to find nowadays.

The period from the 1660s to 1765 saw enormous changes in both the artistic and the technical nature of the Edo publisher's output. The first forty years, up to about 1700, saw hardly any single-sheet prints. It was during this time that the wood-block illustrated books first achieved popular appeal with the middle classes. An extension of these were the *ehon*, picture books with minimal text; by the 1680s larger albums of horizontal prints, usually twelve sheets on a common, often erotic theme, were bound and sold together. During the later 1680s and 1690s single-sheet vertical prints first began to appear. These large *kakemono-e* prints, impressive and effective posters, continued to be produced until 1718, when they were banned by government decree. Some of the early books, the *tanroku-bon*, were roughly hand-coloured by daubing with red lead (*tan*) and green (*roku*), derived from verdigris. The album prints were printed and sold in black and white, *sumi-e*, but have sometimes been hand-coloured subsequently. The *kakemono-e* and other prints between about 1700 and 1715 were often hand-coloured and are known as *tan-e* since the brick-red colour of *tan* often predominated (plate 15).

From about 1715–20 more careful, accurate hand-colouring with more delicate shades resulted in the *beni-e*, so called after the typical *beni* dye, a rose-pink derived from the safflower. *Beni-e* continued to be produced after the large *kakemono-e* were banned, when the smaller *hosoban* format became the norm. From 1720–40 the *beni-e* were often embellished with areas of lustrous black lacquer applied to portions of the design, sometimes accompanied by finely powdered brass-dust sprinkled on to areas spread with glue. These 'lacquer prints' are known as *urushi-e* (plates 23, 24). Then in about 1744, colour began to be applied

17. Toyonobu, *Young man on an ox*, 1750s. *Ōban benizuri-e*. Tokyo National Museum.
The ox carrying the dandified young man playing his flute turns aside to investigate the baskets of tender, leafy shoots harvested by the boys. The scene is a parody on a famous parable of Zen Buddhism.

18. (*Overleaf*) Gakutei, *Fan Bridge by moonlight* from *Views of Mount Tempo (Osaka)*, 1834. *Ōban* colour-printed album sheet. London, Victoria and Albert Museum.

天保山末廣橋月夜の図

24

19. (*Right*) Moronobu, *Lovers*, Early 1680s. *Oban* album sheet, *sumizuri-e*. New York, Metropolitan Museum of Art.
A beautiful and romantic scene from a set of twelve erotic prints. A young *samurai* is embracing a girl beside a stream. The chrysanthemums, lespedeza and autumn grass are emblematic of October.

20. (*Opposite left*) Sugimura Jihei, *Courtesan and Lover,* mid-1680s. Hand-coloured *oban* album print. Chicago, Art Institute of Chicago.
The single curve formed by the lines of the standing courtesan and her reclining, importuning lover, serves to isolate the couple from the maid in the background. The characters of the artist's name can be found incorporated into the patterns of the robes: Sugimura, on the girl's *kimono* and Jihei on the man's sash.

21. (*Opposite above right*) Kaigetsudo Anchi, *Standing courtesan*, 1710s. *Kakemono-e* hand-coloured print. Chicago, Art Institute of Chicago.
This large print with a statuesque pose by a courtesan, resplendent in her striking *kimono,* is typical of the rare prints by the Kaigetsudo artists.

22. (*Opposite*) Kiyonobu, *Standing courtesan with an attendant,* mid-1710s. *Kakemono-e, sumizuri-e*. Chicago, Art Institute of Chicago.
26

by overprinting the black outline keyblock with, initially at least, two colour blocks. These were usually printed in *beni* and another colour, often green, and are the *benizuri-e* (pink-printed pictures) (plates 27, 28). Colouring by hand gradually died out and by 1751 the two colour prints were almost universal. During the 1760s further colour blocks were added, giving three, four or even occasionally five colour prints, until in 1765 multi-block, full-colour prints were achieved.

This early period, prior to full-colour printing, saw some remarkable and original artists. The first major figure that we know by name was Moronobu (active 1670–94). He followed a succession of anonymous artists, who had helped formulate the genre style of painting and book illustration known as *ukiyo-e*. It was Moronobu, however, who consolidated these trends and set the new popular art on a firm footing. After early training in the Tosa style of academic painting in Kyoto and later study under Kano Tanyu, he became the most prolific book illustrator of his day at the very time that the *ukiyo-e* style was developing. His *meisho-ki* guidebooks incorporated scenes from everyday life. He invented the *ehon* picture books, for which the New Yoshiwara and its inmates provided a spicy source of material. He pioneered the production of the albums of prints, some showing everyday scenes, many devoted to erotica. The latter would usually contain at least one or two semi-erotic, more romantic pictures (plate 19) and it was these, together with his well known scenes of townsfolk in settings in and around Edo, which established Moronobu's reputation as the great master of early *ukiyo-e*. He is important also for the enormous influence that he exerted on his contemporaries and followers. Sugimura Jihei (active c.1680–98) worked in a style that mirrored that of Moronobu so closely that for many years he was not recognized as a separate artist. Although most prints and album plates of this era were unsigned, some of Jihei's have his name incorporated into the design.

Over two-thirds of his identified work is erotic and, in this field, he comes close to, some say even surpasses, the quality of Moronobu, although he lacked the innovatory flair and breadth of talent of the master.

During the 1680s, when his first important albums were being published, Moronobu established a school of artists including Moroshige, Morofusa and Tomonobu who also produced a few rare prints. Although Moroshige had pupils in his turn, notably his son Moromasa, the impetus of the direct line petered out and it was left to others to take the Japanese print further.

The first two decades of the eighteenth century saw the production of the impressive large prints of courtesans by Kiyonobu and Kiyomasu and the Kaigetsudo artists. It is important to realize how comparatively large these *kakemono-e* are as this is seldom apparent from reproductions in books. The Kaigetsudo artists are known exclusively for paintings and prints of courtesans, almost invariably standing against a plain background (plate 21). The patterns and cut of the kimono designs seem to have been as important as the girls, who are never named. These prints and paintings were produced and sold from a wayside studio on the route between Edo and the Yoshiwara. Many more paintings than prints have been preserved. The prints are very rare, only twenty-two designs being known, most of them extant in no more than one or two copies, and virtually all of these now reposing in museum collections. Both the paintings and the prints are beautifully and boldly constructed, conveying superbly the coquettish queens of the *demimonde* of the Yoshiwara. They are rightly highly prized and treasured.

The only real rivals to the Kaigetsudo artists for this type of large print were the first masters of the Torii family, Kiyonobu and Kiyomasu. Kiyonobu (c.1664–1729), the son of a *kabuki* actor who also painted the vivid, colourful signboards which hung outside the theatres, moved to

23. Kiyomasu II, *The actor Ichikawa
Monnosuke holding a stage wig,* mid–1720s.
Hand–coloured *Hosoban* print. London,
British Museum.

24. Kiyomasu II, *The actor Matsushima Hyotaro standing before a screen,* mid-1720s. Hand-coloured *Hosoban Urushi-e* print. Cambridge, Fitzwilliam Museum.

25. Kiyotada, *Kabuki dance,* c.1720.
Hosoban tan-e, hand-coloured print. New
York, Metropolitan Museum of Art.
Little is known about Kiyotada but here
he has caught perfectly the exuberant
vigour of the dance performed by the
great actor Ichikawa Danjuro II.

Edo from Osaka in 1687. Living and working among the actors, he knew every nuance of the plays and the theatrical world. This was an exciting time both in the visual arts and in the theatre. Moronobu and Jihei were both at the height of their careers, producing prints of a new power and impact by the use of thick, swirling lines and carefully composed areas of black. In the theatre, the great actor and playwright Ichikawa Danjuro I was taking the *kabuki* audiences by storm with the complexity and sophistication of his plots and his own swashbuckling style of acting known as *aragato.*

Kiyonobu was much influenced by Moronobu and started by illustrating books. By the turn of the century he had developed his mature style and from then until the late 1720s he was an artist of major importance producing work of high quality although not apparently in large quantity. It is postulated that when his father died in 1702, Kiyonobu took over his hereditary position and spent much of his professional career painting *kabuki* bill-boards. Nevertheless he produced some good erotic albums, some excellent *ehon* and, most famous of all, his prints of actors and courtesans (plate 22). The actor prints were designed in two distinct styles and these are also characteristic of the work of his more prolific contemporary Kiyomasu. The first, which was evolved to show the *aragato* style of acting, carried the flamboyant lines of the *kabuki* sign-boards onto the *kakemono-e,* poster-like prints. Plates 15 and 128 demonstrate the conventional characteristics of this style with the 'gourd legs', to give the impression of power and strength, and 'wriggling worm lines' to convey a taut, twisted vigour. The second, quieter, more restrained style was used to illustrate the more elegant, realistic acting of intense, emotional roles typified by *wagoto* (soft stuff) that was typical of the *kabuki* in Kyoto and Osaka. Prints showing this more refined acting are more associated with Kiyonobu but many examples can also be found by Kiyomasu (plate 23).

Kiyonobu died in 1729 and probably ceased designing prints a couple of years before this. Kiyomasu worked from the late 1690s until the mid-1720s. Problems arise because there was at least one other artist, working later in the same style, who signed himself Kiyonobu and more than one who signed Kiyomasu. Where the dates of theatrical prints can be established, it is accepted for convenience that prints signed Kiyonobu between 1729 and 1763 are attributed to Kiyonobu II. The date of Kiyomasu's death is not known but the one or more artists designated Kiyomasu II were designing prints from the mid-1720s to 1763, after which no prints signed Kiyonobu or Kiyomasu are known. The relationships between these various artists remain unclear and have been a matter for endless speculation.

The second generation of Torii print artists included Kiyotada (active c.1718–50) (plate 25), Kiyoshige (active late 1720s to early 1720s) and Kiyotomo (active 1720–40) as well as Kiyonobu II and others. During this period the *hosoban beni-e* and *urushi-e* (plate 24) predominated until

the *benizuri-e* two colour prints came in during the 1740s. By the 1750s a third generation, headed by Torii Kiyomitsu (1735–85), was active. Kiyomitsu worked from the late 1750s for about ten years producing prints of girls and actors, mostly in two colours. In the early 1760s he was one of those who pioneered the three and four colour prints that presaged full-colour printing (plate 29). His contemporary Kiyohiro excelled at two colour *benizuri-e* of particular freshness and charm, often forsaking the stylized Torii actor for the more fashionable modes that were coming in.

Although the Torii line of artists form an important group, they were by no means the only print designers of the first half of the eighteenth century. One of the outstanding men was Okumura Masanobu (1686–1764). His career spanned the time of all the important innovations in print techniques prior to full-colour printing and, by his own account at least, he invented most of them. He was a talented artist who, for a while, ran his own publishing business and, even if he did not himself invent such novelties as the lacquer print, the two colour print (plate 27), the pillar print or the perspective *Uki-e* (plate 12), he certainly did much to promote and consolidate these new techniques. His early work, from the first decades of the eighteenth century, was much influenced by Moronobu and Kiyonobu and includes several albums of erotica. About 1715 he produced hand-coloured *kakemono-e* portraits of girls in an individual style reminiscent of the Kaigetsudo artists. For the next fifty years he was in the forefront of the art, keeping up an output of designs characterized by a gracefulness and a sophisticated wit hitherto unknown. He had followers and pupils, most notably Toshinobu (active 1717–50), an artist of considerable talent who specialized in carefully hand-coloured *urushi-e* of figure studies.

26. Shigemasa, *Spring Festival Dancers*, mid-1760s. Horizontal *hosoban* four-colour *benizuri-e* Private Collection. This delightful picture of the festival dancers, lively but elegant, must come from the era immediately preceding the advent of the multi-coloured prints. The hats are decorated with flowers.

27. (*Left*) Okumura Masanobu, *Girls going to the theatre*, mid-1750s. *Oban benizuri-e* two-coloured print. London, British Museum.
The girl on the right is studying a theatre playbill. The young attendant is carrying a *samisen* box. The poem reads 'Plucking the first tune of the New Year, visiting the theatre on the sly'.

28. (*Right*) Mangetsudo, *Young girl adjusting her hair in a hand mirror*, 1750s. *Hosoban benizuri-e* two-colour print. London, British Museum.
This print is notable for the very remarkable retention of its pink and green colouring.

Shigenaga (d.1756?) was another important artist who worked from about 1720. Like Masanobu he was not restricted to figure prints and actors and he produced some interesting pictures of birds (plate 112) and perspective prints. In about 1730 he pioneered a vogue, later followed by Masanobu and Kiyomasu II, for sets of prints on classical themes, the *Eight views of Omi, Seven Komachi* (plate 31) and the *Tale of Genji*. These used an elegant, archaic style with echoes of the conventions of the Tosa school of painting. In addition to touches of lacquer, metallic dusting and mica, pigment was applied by blowing fine droplets through a small hinged tube, producing a stippled effect, the parts of the print to be left untouched being masked. A stencilled pattern could also be produced in this way.

Shigenaga had as his pupil Toyonobu (1711–85) who, during the 1730s produced some excellent *beni-e* and *urushi-e* figure prints, including triptychs, under the name of Shigenobu. He changed his name to Toyonobu in the 1740s when he fell under the spell of Okumura Masanobu and emulated him by producing some impressive large panels (c.20 × 10 inches) and pillar prints. In the 1750s he produced some beautiful pink and green *benizuri-e* in the large *oban* size (plate 17).

The pretty two colour print (plate 28) brings us face to face with a problem. It is the right-hand sheet of a *hosoban* triptych and its design is almost identical to a triptych by Toyonobu. Plate 28, however, is 'signed' Mangetsudo (Hall of ten thousand moons). Other similar triptychs, bearing the same signature, are copies of Masanobu's work. It seems that Mangetsudo is an entirely fictitious name put on pirated copies of other men's work by an unscrupulous publisher. Certainly Okumura Masanobu frequently inveighed against copyists and forgers in spite of the fact that some of his own early work is based almost line for line on albums by Moronobu and Kiyonobu. In fact borrowing ideas from other artist's designs seems to have been commonplace throughout this period.

One of the artists whose work was widely influential in his own day and which was still being extensively borrowed from a generation after his death was the Kyoto artist, Sukenobu (1671–1750). Working for a different clientele in the old capital, his output consists almost entirely of book illustrations and *ehon* except for a few remarkable erotic albums. He illustrated some two hundred books and is best known for his delightfully graceful pictures of girls, whom he drew seemingly endlessly in any number of activities and settings.

Edo in the early 1760s saw the two colour *benizuri-e*, which had been current for twenty years, edging towards a new era in colour printing. Toyonobu, Kiyomitsu, Kiyohiro and newcomers, the young Shigemasa (plate 26) and Harunobu were beginning to design prints using three, four or occasionally five colour blocks. Okumura Masanobu died in 1764 at the age of seventy-eight. For once he was unable to claim the credit for what was to come.

29. (*Opposite left*) Kiyomitsu, *The actor Onoe Kikugoro*, early 1760s. *Hosoban* four-colour *benizuri-e*. Private Collection.

30. (*Opposite below left*) Okumura Masanobu, *Courtesan and attendant*, mid-1740s. *Kakemono-e* hand-coloured *beni-e*. London, British Museum.
The courtesan is giving instructions to her young attendant, who is holding a love-letter. It is interesting to compare this design with that of plate 33.

31. (*Opposite right*) Shigenaga (attr.), *Kayoi Komachi*, 'Komachi and the Suitor', No. 2 from the set *Seven Komachi*, c.1730. *Hosoban* hand-coloured lacquer-print with metal dusting, mica and blow stippling. Courtesy of Brian Page, Kokoro, Brighton.
The scene alludes to the legendary courtship of the poetess Ono no Komachi by her suitor Fukakusa who kept vigil outside her house for ninety-nine nights, only to die of cold on the hundredth. The picture shows a variant of the *noh* scene. The poem (by Fujiwara Shunzei) reads:—
'I should have realised.
having scored up all those marks
on your mounting block,
the hundredth night is the same:
I see I must sleep alone.'
(trans. D.B. Waterhouse)
This print, apparently unique, is from a rare set which features specially fine hand-colouring and decoration. Two other prints from the set, the *Sekidera* and *Kiyomizu* episodes (see Chapter 8), are in the Royal Ontario Museum, Toronto.

32. (*Overleaf left*) Harunobu, *Collecting insects by lamplight*, c.1768. *Chuban* colour print. London, British Museum.

33. (*Overleaf right*) Harunobu, *Courtesan and attendant*, late 1760s. *Chuban* colour print. London, British Museum.
Compare the design with that of plate 30.

3
Harunobu and the full colour print

The breakthrough to the glories of the multi-coloured print came in with the New Year's celebrations of 1765. This we know because the first prints to use the new techniques were calendar prints. Several interrelated forces, political, technical and financial, combined to make these possible.

Political factors did more to hold back these beautiful and ostentatiously colourful prints than to promote them. The robust and efficient Shogun Yoshimune, who came to power in 1716, found the nation's economy in a parlous state and swiftly issued a series of sumptuary edicts, generally designed to reduce the overall standard of living and especially to limit conspicuous luxury. Amongst the many detailed regulations were restrictions on increasing the complexity, colour and expense of the prints, and these may have done much to prevent the earlier progression to colour printing. Yoshimune retired at about the time that the *benizuri* printing came in. He was succeeded by weak and incompetent Shoguns, who allowed the corrupt but talented Tanuma Okitsugu to dominate government policy from the mid-1760s for over twenty years. The regulations were not rescinded but it seems that a blind eye was turned to quite flagrant breaches of the laws.

As the political climate became easier, technical innovation in printing advanced. The *kento* mechanism to obtain registration of the colours of the *benizuri-e* was well known and has already been described. But a new device was introduced, the *kuiki*. This was a thin wedge of wood which slotted just inside the working edge of the *kento* and allowed extra fine adjustment to the registration. The increased number of blocks, each capable of slight expansion or shrinkage as they became dampened during printing or dried out between runs, and the similar alterations to the heavier paper as it absorbed the pigments, made this essential.

Changes were made in the wood selected for the printing blocks. Previously catalpa wood or, less commonly, the wood of the *hinoki* (Japanese cypress) had been used for engraving. The cherry wood that was now introduced was harder and allowed finer printing. The *masame-gami* paper used hitherto was replaced by *hosho,* a luxurious, thick, soft, absorbent paper that took up the pigments well, withstood the repeated rubbing of the *baren* and allowed the deep impressions of the blind-printing blocks.

34. Harunobu, *Visiting a shrine in the rain,* late 1760s. *Chuban* colour print. Tokyo National Museum.
On the left is part of a *Torii,* the symbolic gateway to a Shinto shrine, behind the graceful figure of the young girl is part of a grove of sacred cryptomeria trees.

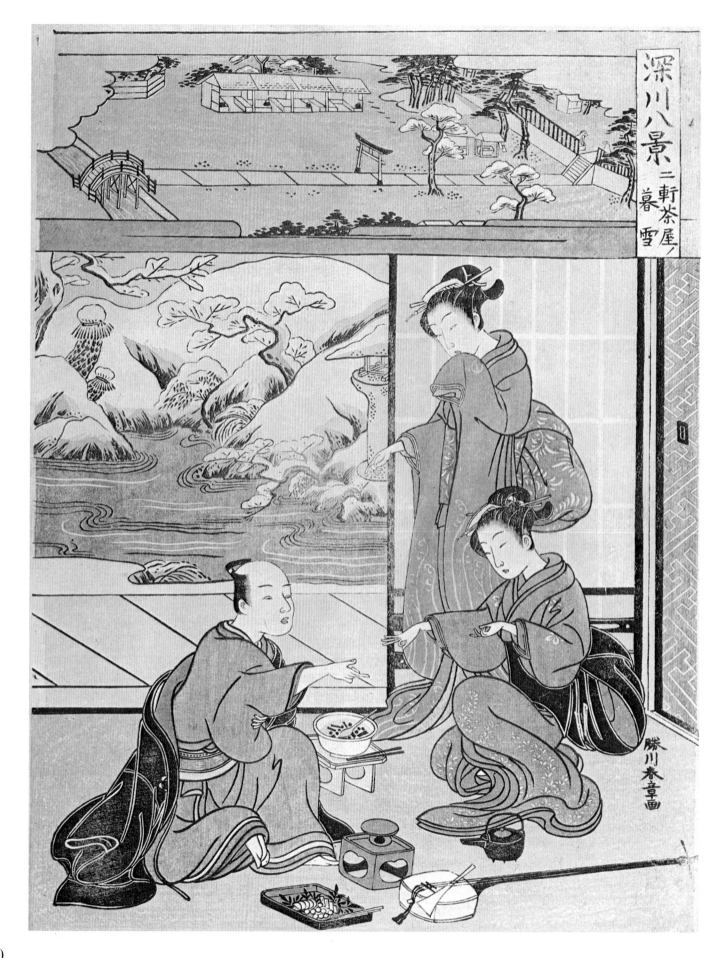

深川八景
二軒茶屋ノ
暮雪

勝川春章画

35. (*Opposite*) Shunsho, *Lingering snow at the Tea-house of the Two Eaves*, from *Eight Views of Fukagawa*, c.1769. *Chuban* colour print. London, British Museum.
Fukagawa was a district of Edo notorious for its unlicenced brothels. The kneeling girl is playing a variant of the finger game *Ken* with her client. The gestures are not those of the usual game and may have erotic significance.

36. Buncho, *The actor Segawa Yujiro as Onna Asahina*, 1772. *Hosoban* colour print. Cambridge, Fitzwilliam Museum.

37. (*Above*) Harushige, *Preparing for the Night*, early 1770s. *Chuban* colour print. Tokyo National Museum.
Within the mosquito netting a young courtesan is killing insects with a taper. Her attendant is asleep and a young man is just entering through some curtains.

38. (*Opposite*) Shunsho, *The Fading Chrysanthemum*, early 1770s. *Koban* colour print. Private Collection.
The chrysanthemum arrangement, with its attached poem, is about to be sent to the elegant courtier Ariwara Narihira. The verse (above) coyly and allusively invites his amorous advances. From the rarer, second set of twenty-four prints showing episodes from the *Ise Monogatari* (page 112).

39. (*Overleaf left*) Sharaku, *The actor Ichikawa Komazo II as Shiga Daishichi*, 1794. *Oban* colour print, grey mica background. London, British Museum.
Shiga Daishichi is a villainous *samurai* who had killed a brave *ronin*, who had defended the rights of the local farmers. The plot tells of the revenge exacted by the *ronin's* two daughters, one a famous Yoshiwara courtesan.

40. (*Overleaf right*) Toyokuni, *The actor Fujikawa Tomokichi II as O-Kaji*, c.1811. *Oban* colour print. Private Collection.
This print is a fine example of Toyokuni's middle period and was doubtless issued to advertise this Osaka actor's debut on the Edo stage.

All these changes and the wider range of special dyes and pigments used were expensive. The initial impetus that led to the introduction of these new techniques was the private commissions of wealthy connoisseurs. Once the breakthrough was achieved, however, no one wanted to revert to second-best and the full-colour print became the norm.

The wealthy dilettanti, the prime movers in all this, were members of literary clubs in Edo, who met together to converse, to compose the snappy, witty, seventeen syllable *haiku* or *kyoka* verse and to dabble in antiquarian and artistic curiosities. These were probably fairly convivial meetings rather than solemn gatherings of learned men, and their members were certainly regular patrons of the Yoshiwara. The *haiku* poet Saren, who was to provide the poems to accompany Harunobu's pictures in a book of 1770 illustrating Yoshiwara courtesans, was the owner of the Miura-ya, a Yoshiwara brothel, and also a member of the Kyosen club. It was this club, more than any other, which is associated with the introduction of the seminal calendar prints, although it was by no means the only one.

In most instances the amateurs who commissioned the prints used professional artists to prepare designs for the block-cutter from their original ideas. By far the most important and influential artist was Harunobu (1724–70). He was probably a member or close associate of the Kyosen club and much of his work contains literary and poetical references, both to contemporary and classical writing. His artistic training is uncertain. He is said to have studied under Shigenaga but his few surviving early works, whether in book illustration or in prints, seem to show the influence of Kiyomitsu and Toyonobu. In 1763–4 he was experimenting, together with Shigemasa and Kiyomitsu, with *mizu-e,* forerunners of the colour prints, using three or four rather insipid, pale colours without the customary black outline. These are almost all illustrations of classical literary subjects. With the calendar prints, however, Harunobu struck a rich vein of inspiration, which he was to explore fully before his death in 1770. His subject was girls. They were pretty, exquisitely feminine, delicate and charmingly posed. Many were courtesans, some were well known beauties of the day. Others were ordinary girls and housewives, seen going about their everyday tasks. Many of his designs have been shown to have been based on book illustrations by Sukenobu. Research has shown links between Harunobu and Sukenobu's family but there is no evidence that they ever met. It is likely, however, that he used Sukenobu's published works as source books, both for the faces, poses and activities of his typical girls and, frequently, for their physical setting. Unlike many of the preceding Edo prints of girls, Harunobu often puts his figures in a fully worked out scene. However much Harunobu plagiarized the ideas of others (and Sukenobu was not the only artist from whom he borrowed – compare plates 30 and 33), the synthesis was all his own.

43

44

お槙
嵐川友吉

豊国画

45

The outcome is frequently delightful.

He was a prolific artist and is estimated to have designed over a thousand prints as well as a large number of book illustrations during his relatively short career. Although mostly working in the *chuban* format, he also used *hosoban* sheets, especially in his earlier years. He was in the first rank of those mastering the challenge of the pillar print, and, towards the end of his career, designed about a dozen *oban* sheets. He sometimes repeated his own designs in different formats.

The calendar prints of 1765–6 and some other privately issued prints carry the *ko* signature and seals of the amateur who commissioned them (plate 144). Surprisingly the name of the publisher is rarely given. Many of these prints were later reissued commercially, often with altered colours and lacking details such as the calendar markings. These reissues had

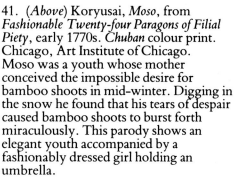

41. (*Above*) Koryusai, *Moso*, from *Fashionable Twenty-four Paragons of Filial Piety*, early 1770s. *Chuban* colour print. Chicago, Art Institute of Chicago. Moso was a youth whose mother conceived the impossible desire for bamboo shoots in mid-winter. Digging in the snow he found that his tears of despair caused bamboo shoots to burst forth miraculously. This parody shows an elegant youth accompanied by a fashionably dressed girl holding an umbrella.

42. (*Above*) Koryusai, *Girl teasing her dog with a samisen*, c.1770. *Hashira-e* colour print. London, Victoria and Albert Museum.

46

the original *ko* signature removed, and often had Harunobu's signature inserted.

After 1766 the role of the private commission diminished in importance as commercial sales to the general public increased. Presumably the unit cost came down with larger editions. Harunobu's output increased to meet the demand. He designed some fine erotica, his seemingly delicate little girls showing every evidence of an enthusiastic sexual forwardness often unexpected by those who know only his more demure prints. The printers went on experimenting with their colours and special effects. The jet-black skies of night scenes (plate 32) were produced by multiple overprinting with the black block. Blind printing and embossing were used both to impress decorative patterns and, occasionally, to outline integral parts of the design.

His influence on his contemporaries was profound but short-lived. Most important of these were Shunsho, Buncho, Koryusai and Shigemasa, who were all to go on to produce significant work in their own styles after Harunobu's death. Direct pupils or followers seem to have been few; they are mostly of interest in debates about unsigned prints in Harunobu's manner and signed prints where there is doubt about the genuineness of the signature and the style is untypical. Such artists include Haruji, Fujinobu, Yoshinobu and Harushige, but their known output is small. Hillier (in *Ukiyo-e Art* No. 26, 1970) managed to track down twenty-eight prints by Yoshinobu. These are attractive, wholly in the style of Harunobu, but of no special distinction. Harushige's work presents other problems. He is known by ten prints, all in the style of Harunobu, signed Harushige (plate 37). These are more than competent but, apart from a slight awkwardness in the setting of the neck on the figures, a tendency to draw the girls rather taller, and a print of an archery booth showing exaggerated perspective, they scarcely warrant detailed interest. Their significance stems from the posthumously published memoirs of Shiba Kokan (1747–1818), a fascinating man of wide-ranging talents, artistic, scientific and literary. Writing some forty years later he confesses that as a young man he had, after Harunobu's sudden death, made imitations of his work, using Harunobu's signature, and that these had fooled the print-buying public. He goes on to say that, to preserve his self-respect, he later assumed the name Harushige. His signed works, therefore, suddenly acquire importance to those attempting to cull Harunobu's *oeuvre* for falsely signed works. Some prints, especially those employing receding perspective, are now widely acknowledged to be the work of Shiba Kokan. The disputes about others will probably never be resolved.

Shunsho, Buncho and Koryusai, all of samurai stock, started their careers in print design during Harunobu's heyday. Shunsho (1726–92) was to go on to specialize in actor prints and some distinguished erotica. Plate 35, however, is clearly in the style of Harunobu's later

48

works of 1768–70. There are other sets by Shunsho from this era. The delightful small prints showing forty-eight episodes from the *Ise monogatari* (see Chapter 8) have settings and costumes which come from the Heian court but the girls step straight out of the world of Sukenobu (plate 38).

Buncho (active c.1765–75) never fell entirely under the spell of Harunobu and his characteristic girls have a unique gracefulness with a typical slant to the eyes and eyebrows and their heads often thrust forwards almost menacingly. The originality of his style is also apparent in his male figures, especially his actor portraits, but they never seem to thrill in the same way as his women. He specialized in *hosoban* actor prints (plate 36) but also produced a few *chuban* prints, mostly relating to the girls of the Yoshiwara (plate 14).

Koryusai (active c.1764–88) started his print career under the direct tutelage of his friend Harunobu and his earliest prints are signed Koryusai Haruhiro. Initially his designs were closely modelled on Harunobu's but he soon developed a distinctive colour sense, often using a dominant scheme of orange and pale green. Before Harunobu died he had been experimenting with *oban* and pillar prints and Koryusai was subsequently to give both these fresh impetus. He was especially skilled at adapting his designs to the awkward shape of the pillar print, *hashira-e*, which, as the name implies, was intended to decorate the wooden pillar supports of a Japanese house. All too often such prints show the browning, staining and fading which this usage promoted. Plate 42 shows Koryusai at his best. The girl has all the fragile beauty of Harunobu at his peak, the cloud-shadowed moon adds interest and balance at the top of the composition and, a typical Koryusai touch, a playful little dog completes the picture. He was fond of drawing birds and animals and was one of the few eighteenth-century artists to produce a substantial corpus of excellent prints of nature studies (plate 110). He is also noted for his many erotic albums (plate 16) and his later *oban* prints of beauties (plate 69).

Shigemasa (1739–1820) was an artist whose career began in the early 1760s with *benizuri-e* (plate 26) and actor prints in the style of Kiyomitsu. He too fell under Suzuki Harunobu's influence during the late 1760s but then went on, most specializing in prints of girls, to make his mark with a distinguished output of books and a relatively small number of admirable prints. He was a gifted teacher and his fine draughtsmanship can be seen reflected in the work of his pupils, Shumman, Kitao Masanobu and Masayoshi. He also indirectly influenced many of the other artists of the next generation.

The few years that saw the flowering of Harunobu's art were a turning point both technically and aesthetically in the progress of the colour print. It was fortunate for the art that such a master arose to put the new techniques on a sure foundation.

43. Toyokuni III (Kunisada), *The actor Ichikawa Danjuro IX*, 1864. *Oban* colour print. Private Collection.

4
Actor Prints

The austere and repressive government edicts from about 1720 to the mid-1760s, which had tended to hold back the development of the colour prints, had also restricted the activities of the *kabuki* theatres. Both triumphantly survived and the partial relaxation under the Tanuma regime led to a renaissance in the *kabuki,* which now flourished as never before. With the concomitant breakthrough into full-colour, the actor prints, which had tended to become rather stereotyped in the later Torii style of the 1740s and 1750s, had a parallel revival.

From about 1767 the full-colour techniques began to be applied to the popular commercial prints instead of being restricted to the private prints of the poetry clubs. Harunobu and Koryusai virtually eschewed the theatrical prints but Buncho, Shunsho and the latter's pupils now took these up and dominated the field for a generation. The typical print was the colour-printed *hosoban* sheet usually issued as a triptych. The actors are shown standing against a simple background and are pictured in their roles. What was new and exciting was that the prints were personal portraits of the actors, easily recognizable by the *kabuki* fans who bought them. It is rare for their names to be given and the actor has to be identified by his features or the *mon* on his costume.

Buncho's actor prints, produced from 1767–75, have a delicate, idiosyncratic style and show a sensitive colour sense. His prints are quite rare and, especially when depicting women, are of a consistently high standard. Both artists collaborated in an important colour-printed book of actor's portraits published in three volumes in 1770 which shows clearly the differences in their styles (plates 45 and 46). Buncho often portrays hauntingly enigmatic women, while Shunsho is better at depicting the more virile male actors.

Shunsho's *hosoban* actor prints are much more commonly encountered. Although sometimes a little repetitious, they are often vigorous and full of the dramatic qualities of movement and power (plate 47). His main period of print production extended to 1785 although he continued to design the occasional print right up to his death in 1792. It was he, perhaps more than any other, who took the actor print and gave the figures personality as well as features. Without Shunsho's talents the actor print might have remained one of standard poses by figures distinguished only by their crests.

He was also the head of an important school of artists. He was a

44. Kunisada, *The actor Sawamura Gennosuke II*, c.1830. *Oban* colour print. Private Collection.

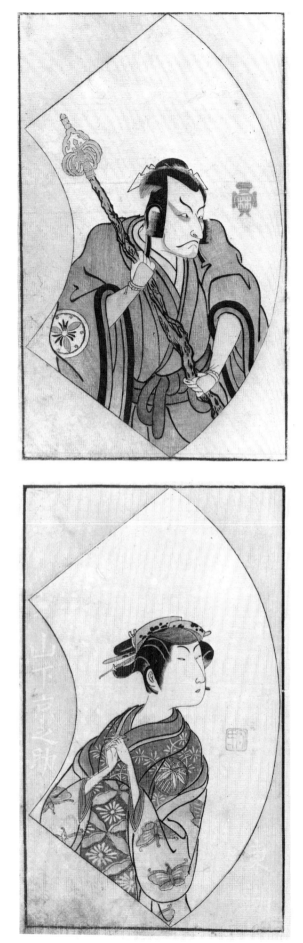

good teacher and was fortunate to have had apt pupils. Shunko and Shunei, both prolific, helped to establish his style as the dominant force in actor prints and much of their work came to equal that of their master. Shunjo (d.1787), Shundo (active 1780–92), Katsukawa Shunsen (active c.1790) and several others all produced some fine prints. Other important pupils, notably Shuncho and Shunro (later to call himself Hokusai) went on to work in other styles and are discussed elsewhere.

Shunko (1743–1812), Shunsho's senior pupil, started to design *hosoban* actor prints in about 1771. He maintained a consistently high standard of competence, often almost indistinguishable from Shunsho himself (plate 49). In about 1787 he had a stroke which partially paralysed his right side. He continued to work, however, learning to use his left hand, and was closely associated with the development of the *okubi-e* ('large head' pictures) of actors.

Shunei (1762–1819), a much younger man, started by following the lead of Shunsho and Shunko and began designing *hosoban* prints (plate 50) in the mid-1780s, continuing until the turn of the century. He had a tendency to give his faces a slight plumpness and to give an increased vividness and accentuation to Shunsho's ability to stamp a personality on his actors.

The larger, *oban* size was used for 'large head' and half-length portraits of actors from the late 1780s. The results are often magnificent. Not that the half-length figure design was new. Shunsho and Buncho's *Picture book of stage fans* had been published nearly twenty years earlier and Shunsho had designed some superb large fan prints with bust portraits of actors in the mid-1770s (plate 154). In *hosoban* format Shunko had also tried his hand at the fan print (plate 153) and in the early 1780s had designed some rare but impressive *hosoban* sheets, divided into two horizontally, with a 'large head' in each half. It was the subsequent combination of the close-up image with the increase in size which made these prints so effective.

Shunko and Shunei were both early instigators of this new style. Shunko's 'large heads' impress with their broad, powerful strokes and simple contours, Shunei's by their more finely drawn intensity and emphasis on emotion (plate 52). Such prints, by either artist, are very rare. The 1790s, however, saw a surge of activity in these larger prints. At the same time an increasing tendency towards realism inspired some remarkable sets of actors.

Toyokuni (1769–1825) and Sharaku, under contract to rival publishers, began to vie with each other to produce prints for the plays of 1794. Toyokuni seems to have started first. He was an established artist and had been producing prints in the style of Kiyonaga and Shuncho for about ten years. His new print series *Portraits of Actors on the Stage* (plate 54) contained nearly fifty individual actors and appeared at intervals between January 1794 and April 1796, a period which also saw the publication of Sharaku's total known output. The actor print was

45. (*Opposite left*) Shunsho, *The actor Matsumoto Koshiro III*, 1770. Colour-printed book illustration from *Ehon Butai-ogi*. 9½ × 6 in (24.5 × 15 cm). Private Collection.

46. (*Opposite below left*) Buncho, *The actor Yamashita Kyonosuke*, 1770. Colour-printed book illustration from *Ehon Butai-ogi (Picture book of stage fans)*. 9½ × 6 in (24.5 × 15 cm). Private Collection.

47. (*Opposite right*) Shunsho, *The actor Ichikawa Ebizo II*, 1772. *Hosoban* colour print. Amsterdam, Rijksmuseum. The large shrimps (*ebi*) on the concentric squares of the Ichikawa *mon* are a part-rebus on his title Ebizo.

48. (*Right*) Shunsho, *The actor Nakamura Nakazo I*, 1770. *Hosoban* colour print. Roger Nyle Parisious Collection.

The actor here is playing the part of the priest Raigo Ajari. He was refused a boon after interceding successfully for the Emperor, who wanted an heir. He retreated to the Mii temple and starved himself to death, his ghost later haunting the temple.

49. (*Far right*) Shunko, *The actor Sakata Hangoro*, early 1780s. *Hosoban* colour print. London, Victoria and Albert Museum.

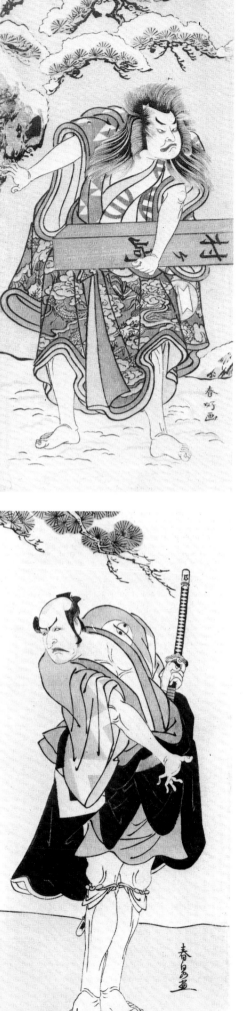

50. (*Right*) Shunei, *The actor Segawa Kikunoju III*, mid-1790s. *Hosoban* colour print. Tokyo National Museum.

51. (*Far right*) Shunsen (Katsukawa), *The actor Arashi Ryuzo*, mid-1780s. *Hosoban* colour print. Cambridge, Fitzwilliam Museum.

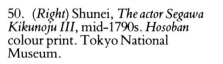

never the same again!

Sharaku remains one of the most mysterious figures of Japanese art. No reliable biographical details are known, no immature works have been found but, during a span of only ten months, he designed some one hundred and forty-three prints, almost all of actors in current *kabuki* performances, in a style almost uniquely his own and apparently fully formed. All his work was published by Tsutaya Jusaburo, the most successful and influential publisher of his day, and many of his early prints are embellished with mica backgrounds (plate 39). These seem to have been an experiment. His first twenty-eight prints, the famous half-length portraits of May 1794, all have mica, often of a glowing, dark purple or steel grey shade. Of the thirty-eight full-length portraits produced for the performances of the seventh and eighth months of 1794, only the eight *oban* prints have mica, the remainder being printed more conventionally and, like most of the rest of his *oeuvre*, in *hosoban* format. His style, which often appears to involve caricaturing the actors, is said by one of the few reliable contemporary sources to have been unpopular. It is certainly not unpopular now. Whether one likes his grimacing portraits or not, they are undeniably powerful and, on those rare occasions when they appear in the sale-rooms, competition for them is fierce.

Linked with the uncertainty surrounding the identity of Sharaku is the even more shadowy figure of Enkyo, who is known by only seven prints produced for plays in late 1795 and early 1796. These are all 'large heads' clearly influenced by Sharaku's style.

What had happened to Toyokuni? Whether he influenced Sharaku more than Sharaku influenced him, there is no doubt that Toyokuni and his pupils were the next to dominate the actor print, although they were in no way restricted to this field. Some of his 'large head' designs come to almost fill the sheet (plates 55, 56) and his half-length portraits show a fine ability to convey the emotional subtleties of the actor's role. Full-length figures, often in two's or three's, set off against a grey ground, became popular in the late 1790s. The *oban* size became the norm, although both Toyokuni and Shunei continued to produce a few *hosoban* prints in the early years of the next century. Almost his only serious rival was his own pupil Kunimasa (1773–1810), who produced some superb work between 1795 and 1805 (plate 57), when he gave up print designing.

For his last twenty years, until he died in 1825, Toyokuni seems to have run a studio workshop to fulfil the continuing popular demand for prints. The list of pupils who subscribed to his tombstone runs to over eighty names, but only a handful of these established themselves sufficiently to have left a substantial quantity of work under their own names. It has to be assumed that many of the others, during their apprenticeship at least, helped to turn out prints under their master's imprint. During this time scenic backgrounds, which had tended to be

52. Shunei, *The actor Ichikawa Komazo II*, 1790. *Oban* colour print. Tokyo National Museum.
The role is that of Ono Sadakura, a villainous cut-throat who has a minor part in the Chushingura story (see page 116).

54. (*Opposite left*) Toyokuni, *The actor Onoe Matsuke as Tonase* from *Portraits of Actors on the Stage*, 1795. *Oban* colour print. Private Collection.

55. (*Opposite right*) Toyokuni, *The actor Onoe Matsusuke as Kudo Suketsune*, the villain of the Soga brothers story (see page 122). 1800. *Oban* colour print. London, Victoria and Albert Museum.

56. (*Opposite below right*) Toyokuni, *The actor Ichikawa Danzo IV as Keya Sonrikusuke*, 1799. *Oban* colour print. Tokyo National Museum.

53. (*Below*) Kunichika, *The actor Bando Hikosakuro V as Akechi Mitsuhide*, 1865. *Oban* colour print. Private Collection. Mitsuhide was a general under Nobunaga in the civil wars of the sixteenth century. Overweening ambition lead him to turn his forces treacherously against his patron, who was slain. He was in turn defeated shortly after by Hideyoshi.

omitted from the *okubi-e* and early *oban* actor prints, began to become more prominent again. Larger teams of engravers and printers, becoming geared to swift mass production of larger editions of the increasingly popular prints, were better able to cope with the increased workload imposed by the more complex settings. Theatrical prints tended to become dramatic scenes with actors. Triptychs became more common again and the 'large head' actor prints were often restricted to private commissions.

Various artists used Toyokuni's name after his death. The artist now known as Toyokuni II was Toyokuni's son-in-law Toyoshige (1777–1835). He started signing his work Toyokuni in 1826. The style of his signature, although usually distinguishable, is not much different from Toyokuni's later signature and has been known to lead to errors of attribution. He sometimes adds the *go* 'Gosotei' to his signature. Toyoshige is the most likely candidate for the postulated position of chief studio artist in Toyokuni's atelier, probably working up his master's sketches for the block-cutters. He was nearly fifty when Toyokuni died and few prints signed Toyoshige are known by him before that date. As soon as he assumed the mantle of his master's name, however, he produced many prints in a style scarcely different from that of the 'late Toyokuni' actors and girls attributed to his master (plate 58). His assumption of the title did not, apparently, find favour with the other senior pupils and he later reverted to signing himself Toyoshige before his death in 1835. In 1844 Kunisada signed several prints 'Kunisada changing to the second Toyokuni' (plate 87) (thereby totally ignoring Toyoshige's previous claim) and thereafter signed all his prints Toyokuni. This signature is almost invariably enclosed within a red cartouche with a yellow border (plate 6). Signing thus he is known today as Toyokuni III. Kunisada's pupil Baido Kunimasa (the third of that name!) took over his master's title in 1846 and began signing himself Kunisada in a similar cartouche (plate 1) and after Kunisada's death used Toyokuni from about 1870, thus becoming Toyokuni IV. His pupil, who became Kunisada III in 1889 is said to have called himself the 'fourth' Toyokuni (i.e. Toyokuni V) late in life. He died in 1920.

Kunisada (1786–1864) started to produce prints in 1809 and went on to become the most important actor-print designer of his day, a position he was to retain until his death over fifty years later. His earliest prints, signed Ichiyusai Kunisada (plate 135), show clearly his debt to Toyokuni's style at that time. About 1813 he began signing Gototei Kunisada (plate 59). In that year he designed the first of a notable and rare set of seven bust portraits of actors against mica backgrounds (a device that had hardly been used since the government ban of 1794). In 1827 he adopted an additional *go*, occasionally signing Kochoro Kunisada (plate 44) until he took Toyokuni's title in 1844. It was his actor prints for which he was most famous in his own day and from which he

must have derived most of his income. It was these very prints, often uninspired and cluttered in design, often poorly and hastily printed, that until recently had led to his being dismissed from serious consideration as a major artist. His early 'large-head' actors and *bijin-ga* and some of his few landscapes have always been admired. However, as his phenomenal output is culled, it becomes more and more

57. (*Top*) Kunimasa, *The actor Iwai Hanshiro IV*, late 1790s. *Oban* colour print. Tokyo National Museum.

58. (*Above*) Toyokuni II (Toyoshige), *The actor Onoe Kikugoro III as a courtesan reading a letter*, c.1830. *Oban* colour print. London, Victoria and Albert Museum.

apparent that throughout his career he continued to design prints which stand out from the humdrum hackwork and which show real quality. Indeed many of his most splendid bust portraits of actors, often no doubt private commissions, stem from the 1850s and early 1860s when he could doubtless rely on pupils and studio artists to fulfil the everyday commitments (plate 43).

Midway through Kunisada's career came the Tempo reforms. The effects of successive government edicts punctuate the entire history of the popular prints. Mostly such laws were ignored or evaded but those of 1842, the Tempo reforms, had considerable consequences for the actor prints. The reforms themselves were a largely ineffectual effort by the well-meaning but inexperienced Mizuno Tadakuni, advisor to the new Shogun Ieyoshi, to deal with the chronic economic problems of the country, which had reached a new low ebb following the renewed droughts and famines of the 1830s. Restrictions on the colour prints were but a tiny proportion of the new regulations that were promulgated. A different system of censorship was devised and the *kiwame* seal was replaced by the seals of individual censors (see page 170). Prints of actors were banned and, from mid-1842 to 1845 no theatrical prints seem to have been produced. Mizuno, the reformer, and Torii Yozo, the much hated Edo city commissioner, who enforced the laws, fell from power and were impeached in 1844 and 1845 respectively. 1845 and 1846 saw a tentative return of prints of actors but the plays and the actor's name and role were never stated openly and the designs were, at least nominally, of a non-theatrical nature. A frequent device was to adapt the popular *musha-e* warrior prints to show the historical figures that starred in the *jidaimono* plays, giving them the features of the actors. Kuniyoshi (1797–1861), already well known for his *musha-e,* was particularly adept at this. Although he had been designing actor prints on and off throughout his career and had produced some good half-length portraits during the five years preceding the ban, his output of quasi-theatrical prints rose from about 1846 onwards, while that of pure *musha-e* diminished. In 1847 the laws were modified and partially relaxed. Two censor's seals now appear and the plays could be more openly illustrated, although the actor's names were still omitted.

The early 1860s saw the death of both Kuniyoshi and Kunisada, and their many pupils began to produce prints under their own names. With the coming of date seals on the prints, problems of dating cease (see Appendix). It once again becomes common to find the actor's name and role prominently displayed. With increasing European trade following the opening of the treaty ports, especially at Yokohama, aniline dyes imported from Germany began to be used on the prints. The results were apt to produce a somewhat garish effect especially when areas of strident red clashed with a vivid shade of purple, a combination that unfortunately seems to have been quite popular in the 1870s and 1880s.

Although the actor prints of these years have usually been universally execrated, it is still possible to pick out effective, powerful designs where the new colours have been used with discretion. The printers had lost none of their art and were still introducing novel effects. One often finds that areas of black, for instance, have been carefully over-printed with a second, lacquer-like black, which was burnished to give a gleaming, lustrous pattern. Most of the artists of this time concentrated on the *Yokohama-e* (see Chapter 10) or prints showing the increasing modernity of urban Japan and the political events surrounding the collapse of the Tokugawa regime and the reinstatement of the Emperor. Although many of these artists also designed actor prints, the man who specialized in *kabuki* and tended to eschew the 'modern' themes was Kunichika (1835–1900). His work followed the pattern of his tutor Kunisada in that he was prolific and that many of his pot-boilers were downright bad, but there can still be found prints that convey the vitality of the stage and the pulsating moments of theatrical climax as the emotional tensions reach their crescendo (plate 53).

59. (*Above left*) Kunisada, *The actor Ichikawa Ebizo VI*, c.1830. *Oban* colour print. Private Collection.
The actor is playing the role of Minase Rokuro who, disguised as a pilgrim seeks to pass a frontier with his young lord Tokuju-maru concealed in the portable shrine on his back.

60. (*Above*) Kuniyoshi, *The actor Nakamura Utaemon IV as Fuwa Banzaemon*, c.1840. *Oban* colour print. Private Collection.

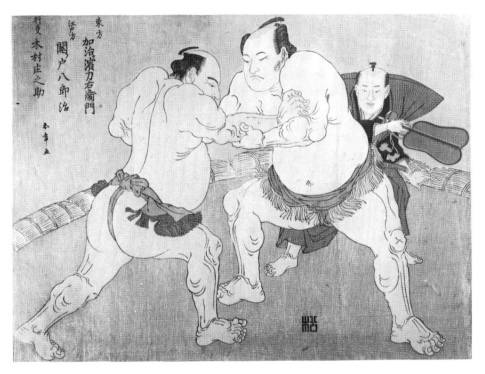

65. (*Left*) Shunsho, *Sumo wrestlers Kajigahama and Sekido*, c.1790. *Oban* colour print. Tokyo National Museum.

Wrestlers

Wrestling, whether in combat (plate 61) or as a spectator sport, not infrequently appears in the prints. Usually shown are the hulking heroes of the *sumo* arena. *Sumo* wrestling was an ancient sport with links with *shinto* ritual. The rules became codified and the participants were mostly professionals. Feudal lords would keep teams of wrestlers to pit against those of other *daimyo*. In Edo special tournaments were held for popular entertainment and wrestlers were graded according to their levels of attainment. Different grades can be distinguished by variations in the hairstyle and the ornate and symbolic decoration of the ceremonial aprons. Since the winner of a bout was he who could either throw his opponent or push him out of the ring, it was an advantage to be heavy. The Japanese tend to be a short race but these wrestlers were tall and massively proportioned.

Several artists drew *sumo* portraits. In the late eighteenth century Shunsho (plate 65) and his followers, especially Shunei, were pre-eminent. In the nineteenth, Kunisada (plate 62) and Kuniyoshi seem to have been most commonly commissioned. The wrestlers are often shown in their ceremonial garb or stripped off for action during a bout. Triptychs sometimes show the formal procession of the wrestlers lining up in front of the circular arena, the grandstands all around packed with a vast, bustling throng of spectators. Less commonly they are shown off-duty in ordinary clothing. Some *kabuki* plays have *sumo* wrestlers as characters (plates 63, 64).

61. (*Opposite above left*) Kuniyoshi, *The fight between Tengan Isobei and Yashiya Arashi*, from *800 Suikoden of Our Country*, c.1830. *Oban* colour print. Private Collection.
The victorious hero is extensively tattooed. His base opponent has darker, hairy skin – a sign of low breeding.

62. (*Opposite above right*) Kunisada, *The Sumo wrestler Abumatsu Rokunosuke*, c.1835. *Oban* colour print. Private Collection.
Note the ceremonial fringed apron. The rope girdle with hanging *gihei* indicate that he is of the highest rank.

63. (*Opposite below left*) Toyokuni III (Kunisada), *Actors in the parts of the wrestlers Iwakawa and Tetsugadate*, 1859. *Oban* colour print. Private Collection.

64. (*Opposite below right*) Eisui, *The Sumo wrestler Tanizo with a sake-cup, behind him the daimyo Yorikane and his mistress Takao*, late 1790s. *Oban* colour print. Cambridge, Fitzwilliam Museum.
The famous *kabuki* ghost play *Kasane* starts with the death of Takao by the hand of Tanizo, faithful retainer of Yorikane. He kills her to release his master, who was so infatuated by her that he refused to take refuge when his life was in danger.

5
Beautiful Women

Prints specializing in pictures of pretty girls, *bijin-ga*, were one of the more popular subjects of Japanese prints. These can be instantly enjoyed for themselves but closer examination will frequently reveal numerous clues which will give the informed viewer enhanced interest and pleasure. A girl's posture, style of dress, hairdo, make-up or actions often had more significance to the print-buying public of Edo than would, at first sight, seem credible. To begin with, there is a fundamental division between prints of courtesans, respectable women and 'actresses'.

Even if we exclude the erotica, an entirely separate genre, prints of courtesans were common from the earliest days until the Tempo reforms of 1842, which virtually eliminated them. Their profession is often obvious from the setting, whether indoors in the Yoshiwara or parading with their cortege of *shinzo* and *kaburo,* but other pointers may also help to identify them. From about 1741, the courtesans were the only women who tied their *obi* with the knot in front. Indoors they mostly went barefoot while ordinary women wore *tabi,* a sort of sock with a division for the big toe. In winter the courtesan wore especially high clogs, *geta.* Many prints carry an inscription, which dispels all doubt. The girl's name may be given together with the name or *mon* of her brothel, or a series title may refer directly or indirectly to the Yoshiwara or other brothel quarter. In any circumstances, a woman with a rolled wad of paper tissues can be assumed to be on her way to a tryst with a lover (plates 14, 92). It is sometimes possible to recognize a famous courtesan by her features, especially in prints of the 1790s when portraiture and the 'large head' and half-length pictures were at their peak. Usually only girls of the higher grades were shown although, as mentioned above, their attendant apprentices, *shinzo,* who were learning the specialized techniques, and *kaburo,* younger girls who were as yet only being instilled with the social graces, may also appear (plate 70). The *kaburo* are often seen in pairs, dressed alike and typically have ornate hair ornaments (plate 69). Lower class prostitutes, usually plying their trade illegally outside the licensed quarters, are occasionally shown.

The tea-house attendants and geisha also had important roles in the amusement centres and licensed quarters. The tea-houses often acted as places of assignation and, in the Yoshiwara itself, the attendants would

66. Kuniyoshi, *Opening shell-fish at Fukagawa* from *Specialities of famous places in Edo*, mid-1840s. *Chuban* colour print. Private Collection.

wait on wealthy clients, ordering food, drink and entertainment and arranging meetings with the courtesans of their choice. The geisha were entertainers, hired by the hour, providing music and dancing to enhance a party atmosphere. They are often shown with a samisen (plate 70), the favourite instrument.

Apart from these professional purveyors of sexual fantasy, respectable women and girls of all classes can often be seen in the prints. The sexual freedom inherent in the lives of the prostitutes did not, of course, extend to the wives and daughters of the townsfolk but, in other respects, women in Edo-period Japan were comparatively free socially, considering the general male dominance of the culture. They are shown on outings to view the cherry blossom, visiting famous shrines, and otherwise just ordinarily out and about, shopping, visiting the theatre or at home engaged in domestic life.

One aspect that is common to almost all the *bijin-ga* is a preoccupation with fashions. This is most obvious in the changes in pattern and style of the kimono and in the hair styles. The kimono, thin and cool in summer, lined or quilted in winter, was the basic dress, gathered above the waist by a contrasting sash (*obi*), wound around the body and tied in a prominent knot. Under-robes can often be glimpsed and much care was given to the colours and patterns of all these so that they should complement each other. The kimono of young, unmarried girls have long, dangling sleeves, extending almost to the ground (plate 28). Up to the middle of the eighteenth century the cut of the garment was longer, especially in front, which meant that when moving, the woman would have to hold her robes up (plates 21, 23). There is no doubt that the styles and patterns of the trend-setters in the Yoshiwara and to a lesser extent the costumiers of the *kabuki*, were faithfully reproduced in the prints and formed an important role for them. What marvellous fashion-plates they are!

Changes in hair styles are important for several reasons. They can sometimes be used as internal evidence to help date a print, since none of the commercial artists could afford to be behind current fashion and some of the changes were, in sophisticated Edo at least, sufficiently universal to make this a useful guide. A comparison of the hair styles in plate 41 by Koryusai with that of the girls in plate 69 by the same artist a few years later demonstrates the changes introduced by the use of the *binsashi*, a flexible internal support for the side 'wings' of the hair. Several prints of the era, about 1775, when this device became popular, deliberately show detailed views of the new style from different angles, including the back (plates 13, 69). This emphasis on showing the intricacies of new styles has led to some of the most admired designs. It is even possible that the beautiful print by Utamaro on the cover would never have been drawn but for the need to give the Edo women a close-up view of the latest hair fashion.

When Harunobu died, in 1770, his style of slim daintiness gradually

gave way to more rounded, solidly built girls. The artists giving the lead were Shigemasa and Koryusai. Shigemasa's best work is to be found in his book illustrations, but his output of prints although small, is highly admired. His main claim to fame is a small series of *oban* prints, each showing two or three geisha. These are usually found unsigned. Koryusai was more prolific. He kept up a steady output of *chuban bijin-ga* and produced some outstanding pillar prints as well as designing prints of children, animals and birds and some notable erotica. By the mid-1770s, the *oban* format began to predominate and this enabled the larger figures to be shown to advantage. Koryusai was commissioned to design a long series of prints under a title that meant *New Patterns for Young Girls* (plate 69). These were fashion plates but the models were the most famous courtesans of the day. His inventiveness sometimes flags but the one hundred and forty prints known contain many attractive designs. Koryusai gave up print design for painting around 1780. His *New Patterns,* however, were so popular that the publishers, probably at the behest of the brothel proprietors, went on to commission first Kiyonaga and later Shunzan to produce further sheets in the same series.

In 1784 the courtesans were featured in a sumptuous album of seven

67. (*Above left*) Gokyo, *The courtesans parading in the Yoshiwara at the New Year,* early 1790s. *Oban* colour print, *beni-girai.* London, Victoria and Albert Museum. Komurasaki of the Tama-ya (House of the Jewel) is shown with her little *kaburo,* who is holding a battledore, and *shinzo,* who is chatting to a young man. The signature proclaims Gokyo to be a pupil of Eishi.

68. (*Above*) Ryuunsai, *Young man and two girls*, late 1780s. *Oban* colour print. British Museum.
Ryuunsai is known by only a few rare prints in the style of Kiyonaga.

青楼名君自筆集

double-*oban* prints by Kitao Masanobu. Each sheet shows two courtesans of the highest class at ease with their attendants. On the sheet was a verse written in the courtesans' own calligraphy, thereby drawing attention to their aspirations to culture and literacy (plate 70). These may have been issued as single sheets the year before the album appeared. At least two editions were published, the second having different colours and omitting the address of Tsutaya, the publisher, over his seal. In these pictures the girls are more robust and solid than a decade earlier. They are also becoming taller, a tendancy which seems to increase gradually over the next fifteen years. Kitao Masanobu's large prints, using the technical resources of his printers to the limit, brought new inventiveness and set higher standards. He did not, however, follow them up, but soon forsook print designing to follow his bent as an author, at which he had considerable success.

The man whose influence most pervaded the 1780s was Kiyonaga (1752–1815). He had been producing actor prints and illustrating novelettes since 1770 but it was not until about 1781 that he found his

70. (*Above*) Kitao Masanobu, *Courtesans at leisure* from *The Autographs of Yoshiwara Beauties* (second edition), mid-1780s. Double *oban* colour-printed album plate. London, Victoria and Albert Museum.

69. (*Opposite*) Koryusai, *The courtesan Mandayu watching her attendants playing dice* from *New Patterns for Young Girls*, mid-1770s. *Oban* colour print. London, Victoria and Albert Museum.

characteristic style of *bijin-ga*. For about six years thereafter he poured out a wealth of attractive prints, almost all of women and girls, in a style which has never lost favour (plates 1, 71). Indeed in 1896 Fennollosa could write of him '. . . a man who, all things considered, is to be regarded as the central figure of *Ukiyo-e*. All up to his central date is a rising curve; all afterward the gradual descent of decay.' Such views were echoed by several of the early commentators but, although his place as the dominant force of his time is undoubted and secure, he is no longer regarded as such an unassailable pinnacle of the whole art. Lane wrote recently 'Indeed, for all his perfection, there is a certain dullness about much of Kiyonaga's work, and the viewer may well find himself turning in relief from this persistent perfection to less impeccable but more human contemporaries such as Choki, Utamaro and even Shuncho.' What, then, is it that Kiyonaga achieved that constitutes such perfection? To the European eye at least, the answer lies in the proportions of his figures. Shigemasa's geishas have been praised for realism – they look like real Japanese women, a little short and slightly dumpy. Utamaro and Eishi, who came later, have been both praised and criticized for their improbably tall, mannequin-like girls. Kiyonaga, consummate artist, blessed with fine printers and engravers, came into his own with women proportioned just right for the Western ideal. He is most noted for his *oban* diptychs and triptychs, a format which he did much to popularize and which gave his compositions a much larger spread. His backgrounds and settings are worked in considerable detail and in his outdoor scenes he managed to capture the atmosphere of the open air. Many of his smaller, *chuban* prints are also delightful and sometimes seem to be unduly neglected by comparison with his larger, more impressive works. Towards the end of the 1780s Kiyonaga, in his role of heir to the Torii line, concentrated on actor prints, a field in which he never excelled. Although he lived on to 1815, his print output after 1790 was small.

Kiyonaga's style, however, had attracted followers and imitators. Shuncho, Shunzan, Shumman, Toyokuni and Utamaro all fell under his spell during their formative years. Shuncho (active 1780–95) modelled himself so closely on Kiyonaga that frequently only the signature tells them apart. He seems condemned to second rank because his art is derivative, although in every other respect he is the equal of his master. In his *shunga* he is even generally acknowledged to be the greater artist. Shunzan produced competent work in much the same style but fewer prints by him are known. Shumman's prints are also few in number but he managed to transcend the uniform type and imbue his prints with an elegant atmosphere hitherto unknown. His most important prints employ a restricted palette, found also in prints of this time by Shuncho and Eishi, where predominant greys and greens are enlivened by small touches of pastel shades. This *beni-girai* (red-avoiding) scheme is surprisingly effective, the general restraint high-

71. (*Opposite left*) Kiyonaga, *Girls preparing for the evening's entertainment at Yanagibashi restaurant*, late 1780s. *Oban* colour print, one sheet of a pentatych. London, British Museum.

72. (*Opposite above right*) Shuncho and Shunei, *Two girls and an actor*, late 1780s. *Oban* colour print. Kansas City, Nelson-Atkins Gallery.
A collaborative design. Shuncho drew the two girls and Shunei the young man, who is either an actor or an effete young dandy. His forelocks have been shaved and the bare portion is covered by a patch of cloth in the style of the female impersonators of the theatre.

73. (*Opposite below right*) Shumman, *Girls gathering bush-clover*, late 1780s. *Oban* colour print, *beni-girai*, one sheet from a hexatych. London, British Museum.
Representing the Crystal river of Noji with its associated poem 'Tomorrow we shall return to the crystal river by the path where the bush-clover abounds, and, fording the stream, cause ripples that cradle the moon'. (See page 87).

74. (*Overleaf left*) Utamaro, *Girls examining a scroll* from *Celebrated beauties compared to the Chushingura*, c.1800. *Oban* colour print. Cambridge, Fitzwilliam Museum.
A parody of Act VI of *Chushingura* (see page 166). The girl with her robe open to the waist represents the young *samurai* Kampei who redeems himself by committing ritual suicide and is shown the scroll that is the covenant of the forty-seven loyal *ronin* before he dies.
From an album of Utamaro prints collected together by Edmond de Goncourt.

75. (*Overleaf right*) Toyokuni, *Two girls and a youth on a beach*, mid-1780s. *Oban* colour print, mica sheen on the sea-shells, centre sheet of a triptych. Private Collection.

76. (*Above*) Eishi, *Girls strolling by Takanawa beach*, late 1790s. *Oban* colour print, one sheet of a triptych. Tokyo National Museum.

77. (*Above right*) Choki, *Sunrise at the New Year*, c.1794. *Oban* colour print, dark mica on sky. London, Victoria and Albert Museum.
The glowing red of the rising sun is contrasted against the dark sky. The plant *Adonis Sibirica* on the stone water butt is associated with the New Year, good fortune and long life.

lighting the few traces of colour used. Such prints may have been produced to comply with government restrictions on the colour used in the prints in edicts promulgated as part of the Kansei reforms of 1787–1790. Shumman's most famous work is a hexatych, each sheet showing one of the 'crystal' rivers with its identifying attributes (plate 73). Even single-sheets from this are rare, especially in the first edition, issued about 1787 by the publisher Fuchisen. A later edition, about 1790, published by Tsutaya used stronger colours. The figures show Shumman's debt to Kiyonaga but the flavour of the whole composition has an added refinement. Shumman went on to specialize in *surimono*, (plates 112, 148) illustrated albums of verses and literature, leaving us tantalizingly few of his full-size prints.

Toyokuni is noted for his skill at selecting the most popular style of the moment and recreating it in his own works. His important place among the actor designers has already been noted in the previous chapter. In *bijin-ga* his mentors were first Kiyonaga and Shuncho, then Utamaro and Eishi. He started in the late 1780s and was active throughout the first quarter of the nineteenth century. His ability has tended to be disparaged by those who find it difficult to classify him among the heterogenous groups of artists working for the commercial publishers of the day. Since the *ukiyo-e* 'school' was hardly a school of art in the accepted sense, Toyokuni must have seemed like the ideal artist to his publishers, who could commission a quiet summer scene on the beach (plate 75) or a startling actor print (plate 56) and obtain first class designs to order. In his hey-day in the 1790s, his only serious rivals in popular acclaim were Utamaro and Eishi.

If the 1780s saw perfectly proportioned, stately beauties, relaxed in

tranquil settings, the 1790s saw an increase in the awareness of their sensual qualities. This, coupled with the trend toward the 'large-head' and half-length figures already noted in the actor prints of this era, led to portraits of women where individual character assumed greater importance. The major exponent of this was Utamaro. Utamaro was almost the same age as Kiyonaga but his original talent was slower to germinate and his most famous masterpieces were not produced until the latter had virtually ceased work. He had designed a few un-distinguished actor prints using the name Toyoaki in the late 1770s. The 1780s saw him working in the prevailing manner, producing diptychs and triptychs which, had he stopped thereafter, would have left him with the reputation of an interesting and slightly individual follower of Kiyonaga. These first mature works can be distinguished by the signature, a carefully drawn Utamaro, the first character with a shortened 'tail', the whole followed by the suffix *ga* (meaning 'drawn'). He did not stop there, however, but went on throughout the 1790s and early 1800s leaving us a legacy of closely observed pictures of Japanese womanhood that has never been surpassed. With the *bijin-ga* it is rarely possible to be as certain of the dating as it is with the actor prints although a few prints at the end of his life carry date seals. With Utamaro's prints it is therefore useful to bear in mind some of the pointers that help trace his development. From the ninth month of 1790, prints passed by the censor carry a *kiwame* seal, although its absence does not necessarily mean that a print predates 1790 (some seem to have slipped through the net). In about 1792 Utamaro changes the character following his signature from *ga* to *hitsu*. The opulent mica backgrounds so effectively used by Utamaro, Eishi, Sharaku and Choki appear to

78. (*Above left*) Eisui, *The courtesan Yaso-oi of Matsuba-ya (Pine Needle House) with a camellia*, late 1790s. *Oban* colour print. Tokyo, National Museum.

79. (*Above*) Eiri (Rekisentei), *Passing a love-letter*, late 1790s. *Oban* colour print. Cambridge, Fitzwilliam Museum.

80. (*Overleaf left*) Utamaro, *The courtesan Kisegawa of the Matsubaya (Pine Needle House)*, from *Seven Komachi of the Green Houses*, c.1795. *Oban* colour print. Cambridge, Fitzwilliam Museum.

81. (*Overleaf right*) Utamaro, *The street corner girl* from *A Collection of Love Poems*, c.1795. *Oban* colour print. London, British Museum.
The poem reads: 'To the woman of the street corner dark is the road of love; in the dusk stands a figure draped in black; O how heart-breaking to her that she must stand with face exposed'. (Binyon).

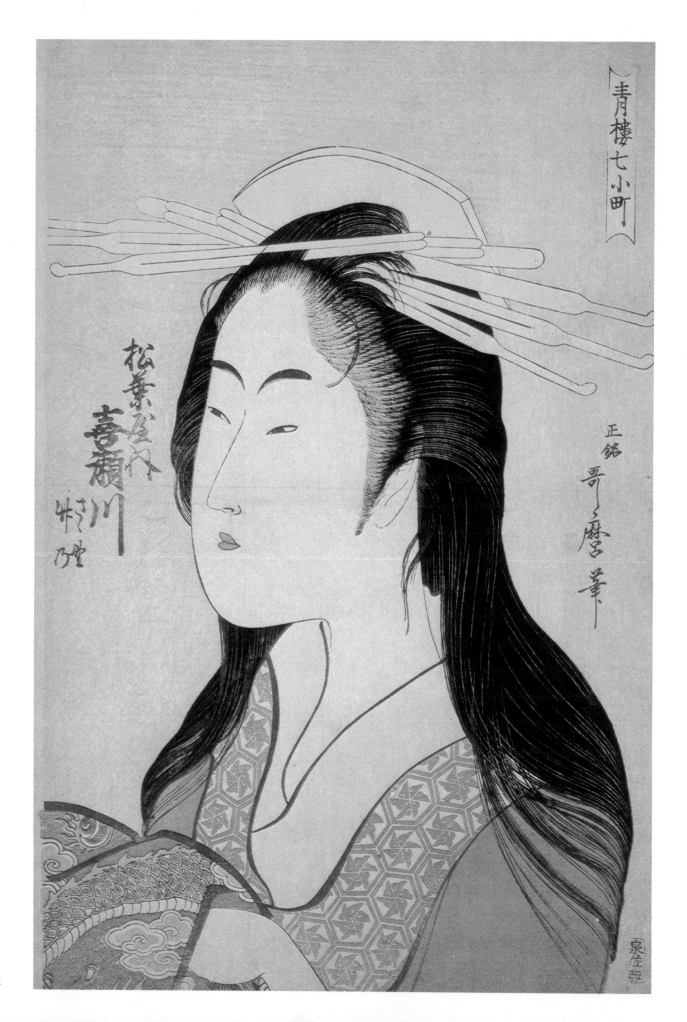

青楼七小町

正銘
哥麿筆

松葉屋内
喜瀬川

74

82. Kiyomine, *Preparing to send a letter*,
mid-1800s. *Oban* colour print. London,
British Museum.
The girl is moistening the paper with her
tongue, the easier to detach it from the
roll. The letter is an acceptance of an
invitation to attend the theatre. The
printing is unusual as the keyblock outline
for the flesh is printed in a pale reddish-
brown instead of the customary black.

have been banned in the eighth month of 1794. Touches of mica had
been used to embellish the finer books and prints well before this,
but the larger expanses used by these artists were probably only
produced for at most two or three years before the ban. This technique
then disappears until a few prints in the 1800s. Prints with a flat,
yellow background came in around 1793, and in 1795, after the ban on
mica, yellow backgrounds with a sprinkling of brass dust had a vogue
(plate 84). From about 1795 Utamaro occasionally prefixes his signature
shomei, (genuine) with a *honke* (original house) seal (plate 106). Prints
on a flat grey ground also seem to date from about 1795 onwards.
More hints can be obtained from subtle changes in the signature and
attention to hair styles and the relative profusion of hair ornaments. It
can readily be appreciated that these factors, even in combination, can
give only an approximation and much of the dating comes down to
educated guesswork.

These problems apart, Utamaro's prints remain deservedly popular.
Most admired are the mica-background bust portraits. Some of these
are pictures of known celebrated beauties of the day, some are
anonymous character portrayals in which he specifically sets out to
discriminate between girls of different temperaments. He obviously
recognized that such an approach was a novelty and often signed these
'Utamaro the physiognomist'. Among the best known yellow background prints is the sequence of twelve prints showing the activities
of the courtesans of the Ogi-ya (House of the Fan) throughout the
twenty-four hours. As usual the fashions are prominent. The girl in
plate 84 has the 'butterfly' hair style popular between 1794 and 1798.
Typical of this set of prints, she shows the trend towards tall, slim
elegance, enhanced here by the foil of her shorter attendant bending to
adjust the lantern. Half-length sets of famous lovers, some masterful
triptychs, a group of pictures of the wild woman Yama-uba and her
adopted 'infant Hercules' Kintoki and many others confirm Utamaro's
place among the greatest masters of the colour print. He died in 1806
and only in his last few years do we detect any falling off in his
originality. This is compounded, as in the case of Harunobu and
Harushige, by some uncertainty about the authorship of some of these
later prints. One of his pupils, who came to be known as Utamaro II,
undoubtedly produced prints signed Utamaro after his master's death.
Some of these bear date seals that clinch this. What is less certain is
how many of the undated prints of the period are his. His reputation is
not high and the tendency is, of course, to look at such a dubious print
and, if one likes it, to assign it to Utamaro I and, if not, to allocate it to
the pupil.

Other artists producing *bijin-ga* in the 1790s include Eishi, his followers, and Choki. Eishi (1756–1829), a wealthy *samurai* of noble
lineage, produced prints in a notably elegant style. About 1790 he used
the restricted colours of the *beni-girai* to great effect. A set of nine

triptychs of *Genji à la mode* are especially noteworthy. These show girls in the most up-to-date fashions in settings related to the tenth century romance. His most typical works, however, show courtesans set off against a yellow background. In his striving for elegant effect, his tall, willowy girls vie with those of Utamaro (plate 76). He was fortunate in his pupils and followers. Eisho, Eisui, Chokyosai Eiri and Rekisentei Eiri are the most notable. But their work, although frequently of a high standard, is scarce and they and the other pupils, whose prints are even rarer, were probably amateurs. Choki is of interest on two counts. The first, and more important, is that among his output of pleasing and competent but otherwise unremarkable prints are a group of half-a-dozen masterpieces. The second is the confusion brought about by his change of name. It is now thought that he first called himself Hyakusen Shiko and illustrated books and designed some prints during the 1770s and early 1780s. Some time between 1785 and 1789 he changed his name to Choki, only to revert to Shiko in 1796, subsequently changing back, yet again, to Choki in 1801. Some hold that prints signed Shiko after 1796 are the work of a pupil of Choki, on whom he bestowed his discarded art-name, and that these should therefore be designated Shiko II. The handful of superb prints for which he is chiefly noted were produced about 1794 and are all signed Choki. As is so often the case with the most impressive prints of this era, they were published by Tsutaya Jusaburo. Mostly half-length figures against a background often embellished with mica, they have a haunting quality of 'time stood still', a captured moment of tranquillity (plate 77).

After Utamaro's death no single artist had the forceful talent and originality to dominate the field of *bijin-ga*. His pupils had none of the magic touch of their master even though each in his turn occasionally produced some pleasing prints. Kikumaro was probably the best (plate 85). He changed his name in 1804 to Tsukimaro and continued to produce prints until 1818. The adherents of other studios began to produce good prints. Kiyomine (1787–1868), a pupil of Kiyonaga, produced some fine work (plate 82) but he was never prolific and, when Kiyonaga died in 1815, he had to assume duties to the *kabuki* as head of the Torii tradition, changing his name to Kiyomitsu II. Kashosai Shunsen, a pupil of Shunei, worked between 1804 and 1820, designing prints of women (plate 83) and, later, some distinctive landscapes, finely printed in pastel shades. The most flourishing artists, though, were Eizan and, a little later, Eisen who had studied with the former's father Eiji, a painter in the Kano style. They have no connection with the school of Eishi. Their careers extended over more than a quarter of a century and saw great changes in women's fashions.

Probably most striking are the new hair styles. From the late 1790s and throughout the early years of the nineteenth century a large, bouffant hair style dominates, appearing rather like an off-balance balloon at the back of the head (plate 85). By about 1810 the light

83. Shunsen (Kashosai), *New Year in the Yoshiwara*, 1805. *Oban* colour print. Private Collection.
Behind the emblematic arrangement of pine and bamboo can be seen a *manzi* dancer, lifting his lion mask, and a flautist. Above, the rope with hanging paper strips, ferns and straw pendants is also traditional at the New Year. This can be seen repeated in the pattern of the *kimono* of the seated courtesan.

84. (*Overleaf left*) Utamaro, *The hour of the Cock* from *Twelve Hours of the Green Houses*, c.1795. *Oban* colour print. London, British Museum.

85. (*Overleaf right*) Kikumaru, *The courtesan Ainare preparing for the tea-ceremony*, c.1800. *Oban* colour print. London, Victoria and Albert Museum.

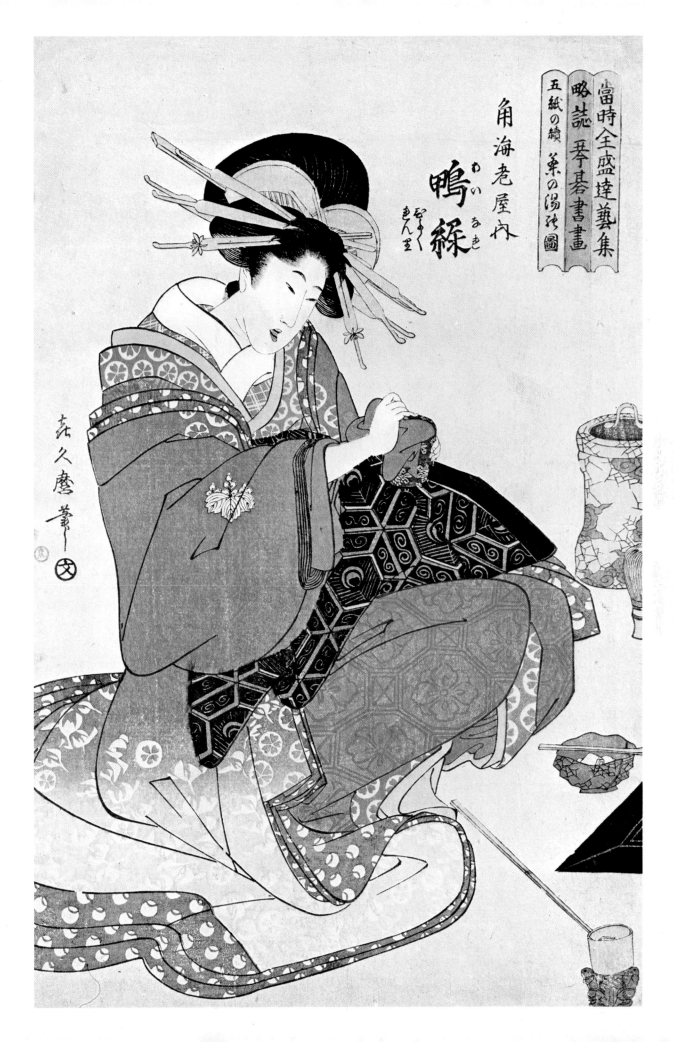

当
時
全
盛
達
藝
集

略
誌
琴
碁
書
畫

五
紙
の
續
菓
の
湯
沸
圖

角
海
老
屋
内

鴨
綠

86. Eizan, *The courtesan Misado of the Tama-ya* (*House of the Jewel*), early 1810s. *Oban* colour print. Private Collection. From a set of seven analogues to the life of the poetess Komachi (page 112). This print refers to the Kiyomizu episode, the spray of flowering cherry providing the link with Kiyomizu temple, famous for its groves of cherry trees.

87. (*Opposite*) Toyokuni III (Kunisada), *Girl amid autumn leaves* from *Lucky Days from a Decorative Calendar*, 1844. *Oban* colour print. Private Collection.

wooden combs that made up the hair ornaments became so profuse, especially with the courtesans, that it frequently makes them appear top-heavy. At the same time fashion decreed an alteration in posture that, to our eyes, makes the women seem almost deformed. In its most exaggerated form this involved an awkward hunching of the back so that the kimono rides up about the neck. The girls of, say, 1820 appear ungainly compared to those of a generation earlier. This fashion made it more difficult to design an attractive picture but some artists adapted skilfully to the changes and many fine prints can be found.

A more serious problem was a decline in the technical quality of the prints. This was more relative than absolute, as many prints continued to be carefully engraved and printed. Many more, however, seem to have been poorly printed with blurred, worn blocks, smudged colours and poor registration. This may have arisen from increased demand and larger editions. It has been suggested that this indicates that the popularity of the prints had percolated downwards to a less refined class of purchaser, who was less discriminating about quality. While this may be true, it is important to realize the political and economic changes that were occurring. It has already been noted that following the austere regime of Yoshimune a partial relaxation occurred during the easy-going, corrupt era of Tanuma. Tanuma was dismissed in disgrace in 1787. The treasury was empty and a succession of poor harvests and natural disasters throughout the 1780s led to widespread famine, poverty and general unrest. The reforming zeal of the new regent, Sadanobu, harked back to the policies of Yoshimune and led *inter alia* to the censor's seals on the prints in 1790. An austerity programme throughout the 1790s was coupled with the good fortune of a series of excellent harvests. The early 1800s saw an increasingly prosperous population chafing under an imposed frugality which was finally relaxed by the actions of the Shogun Ienari and his associates. Ienari (1773–1837) had been a minor during much of the period of reform but, on coming to power, he showed himself to be a dissolute voluptuary. Many of his debauched companions were elevated to positions of responsibility, and corruption and lavish extravagance became the rule. The citizens of Edo started to go on a spending spree and there was a great upsurge in entertainments of all kinds. The theatres and brothels flourished as never before and prints about them were called for in increasing numbers. Small wonder that the publishers went on printing until the blocks wore out if the editions sold. The bubble of prosperity did not really burst until the 1830s when there was a further outbreak of poor harvests, famine, disease and civil strife. It is within this context that the prints have to be judged.

Eizan and Eisen were both affected by the changes in posture and hair styles. Eizan (1787–1867), active from 1804 to 1829, had the advantage of starting much earlier than Eisen; his first prints, which

were still influenced by Utamaro and were designed before the new fashions were fully established, were his best. For a few years he became the leading artist of *bijin-ga*, producing tall, swaying beauties created with long, curved brush strokes (plate 86). Eisen (1790–1848) began to design his typical standing courtesans in about 1821 and the curves of Eizan gave way to compositions made up of short, straight lines showing the increasingly stooping, 'hunchbacked' women, who all seem to be in the grip of intense emotion. In 1823 for three or four years he started to produce some striking half-length portraits of *geisha* (plate 89). In 1829 he started quite a vogue by designing prints coloured almost entirely in different shades of *berorin*, a new, blue pigment. These are known as *aizuri-e*. His pupil Teisei Sencho continued to produce prints of courtesans in the same style and Eisen became increasingly involved in landscape prints (plate 107) and *kacho-ga* (plates 121, 131).

The work of Toyokuni's pupils was so closely linked with the *kabuki* that the majority of the prints depicting women were, in fact, actors in female roles. However, Kunimasa (plate 88), Kuninao (1793–1854), Kunimaru (1794–1829), Toyoshige, Kuniyasu (1794–1832) (plate 92) and others all designed occasional *bijin-ga* and Kunisada and Kuniyoshi both produced some notable work. Some of Kunisada's earliest prints are excellent. These often show *geisha* or girls from the unlicenced and illegal brothel areas that were springing up in Edo and he obviously took great care over these designs at the time when he was trying to establish himself as an independent artist. He was to concentrate on the theatre for most of his career but, following the government edicts of 1842 banning pictures of courtesans and actors, he continued his output of graceful and charming *bijin-ga* (plates 87, 91). Half-length portraits of actors in female roles, unnamed to comply with the ban but recognizable by their features, contributed some of his best pictures of women during the late 1840s and 1850s. Like Toyokuni before him, however, Kunisada was overtaken by his own success. Much of the work for his prodigious output must inevitably have been done by the helpers and students of his studio and this resulted in stereotyped prints of little merit. It is really only in recent years that more careful study of his previously disdained *oeuvre* has shown the considerable numbers of high quality prints that may be found among the dross. As the leading figure design artist of his day he sometimes collaborated with Hiroshige, Kunisada providing the figures and Hiroshige the scenic backgrounds (plate 6).

Kuniyoshi, who could turn his hand successfully to any subject, produced some excellent *bijin-ga*. The resulting prints were often issued as sets. Plate 66 comes from a set of prints showing famous places in Edo, plate 192 from a series linked to the different provinces of Japan. Robinson, in his monograph on Kuniyoshi, lists over seventy further sets devoted to women. With his penchant for legend and history, Kuniyoshi often shows the famous heroines of the past and

88. (*Top*) Kunimasa, *A geisha restringing her samisen*, late 1790s. *Oban* colour print. Tokyo, National Museum.

89. (*Above*) Eisen, *Two contemporary beauties* from *Forty-eight Fashionable Skills*, mid-1820s. *Oban* colour print. London, Victoria and Albert Museum.

is skilful at conveying their characters and temperament.

During the 1860s and 1870s the print artists returned to the bombast of the *kabuki* and the novelties coming out of the European trading centre at Yokohama, but towards the end of the century there was a mild resurgence of the *bijin-ga*. This seems to have been more of a backwards glance at what had gone before than a conscious effort to provide pictures of current beauties. Yoshitoshi seems to have initiated this with his *Thirty-two types of women* of 1888, each personifying one of the preceding *nengo* or historical eras (plate 90). Toshikata (1866–1908) followed these in 1893 with his *Thirty-six Beauties* and Kiyochika (1847–1915) used the same theme for a fine set of triptychs published in 1895. These went under the title *Hana moyo* (Floral designs), and show half-length or reclining girls dominating the large spread of the three sheets. Toshihide (1863–1925) designed a set of twelve prints, *Bijin junishi* in 1901, one for each month of the year, showing girls in the fashions of the *Genroku* era (1688–1703). Throughout the 1890s and early 1900s Chikanobu (1838–1912) was producing a series of triptychs devoted to the elegant pastimes of the noble ladies of the revived Japanese court. These, as in so many of the prints of this era, often demonstrate magnificent *tours de force* in the technical quality of the printing. When the decorative qualities of the printing overwhelm the sometimes weak designs the results are, to modern taste, too sugary, but fine prints continued to be made.

90. (*Above left*) Yoshitoshi, *Courtesan of the Kaei Period* (1848–53) from *Thirty-two types of Woman*, 1888. *Oban* colour print. Tokyo, National Museum.

91. (*Above*) Kunisada, *Fashionable beauty with silk-winding machine*, 1842. *Oban* colour print. Private Collection.

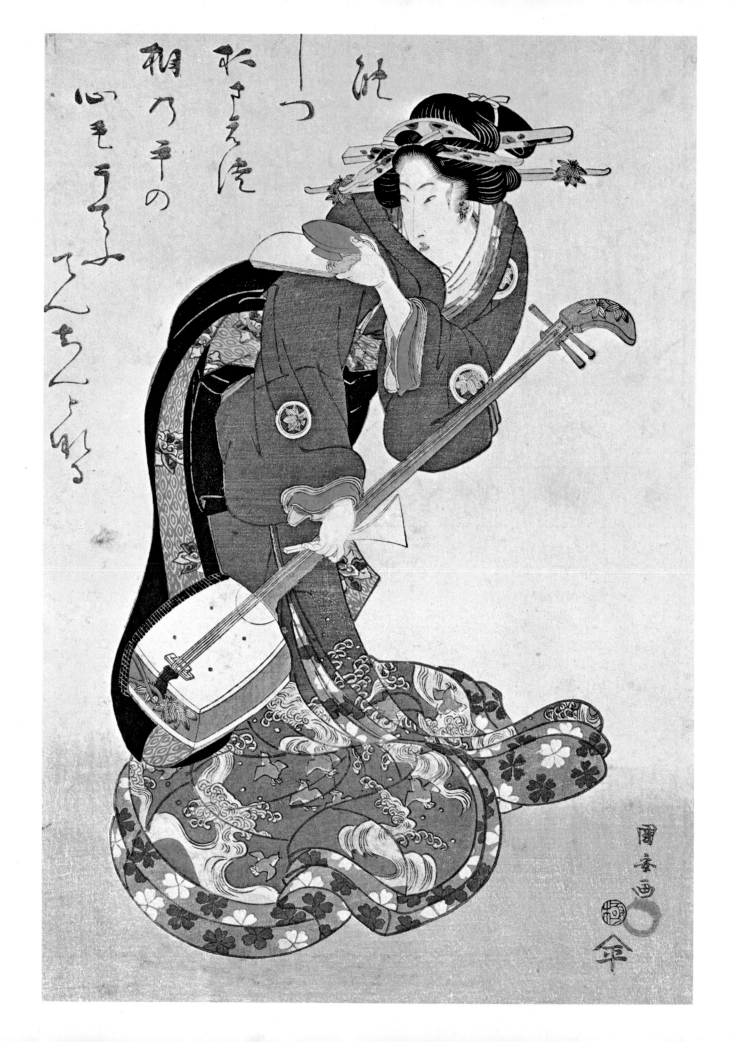

93. (*Above*) Kuniyoshi, *Fuji on a fine day, seen from Edo Bay* from *Thirty-six Views of Fuji seen from Edo*, c.1843. *Oban* colour print. London, Victoria and Albert Museum.
Another, presumably earlier, version carries a poem in the sky above the bird.

94. (*Left*) Toyokuni II (Toyoshige), *Improving weather at Enoshima* from *Eight Famous Views*, mid-1830s. *Oban* colour print. London, Victoria and Albert Museum.
The little island of Enoshima was connected with the mainland, at low tide, by a sandy causeway.

92. (*Opposite*) Kuniyasu, *Girl with Samisen*, c.1830. *Oban* colour print. London, Victoria and Albert Museum.

6
Landscape Prints

Landscape painting has an important place in the history of Far Eastern art. In Japanese prints, however, landscape designs tended to break away from the traditional, Chinese inspired, idealized scenes and concentrate on topography. They seem, in part, to have served the functions of picture-postcards or the snapshots of the modern tourist. Moreover, few of them are purely landscapes, the majority showing figures as a more or less important subsidiary of the design. The seasons and weather were important to the Japanese and often great care was taken to create the atmosphere of, say, a hazy summer day or a crisp autumn morning. The hey-day of the landscape prints was the period from 1820–60. By then, experiments with 'Western' perspective had amalgamated with more traditional oriental styles, resulting in prints which the European eye can grasp instantly with pleasure. It is easy to like the landscapes.

The prints were often prepared in sets. Commonly encountered are the *Eight views, Six crystal rivers, Fifty-three views of the Tokaido, Sixty-nine views of the Kisokaido* and variously numbered sets of views of the provinces, of Fuji, and of famous localities in and around the cities, especially Edo. The *hakkei, Eight views,* is a conventional grouping, based on an older Chinese tradition, and became especially linked with Lake Omi (also called Lake Biwa). The views are: 1. Autumn moon at Ishiyama; 2. Lingering snow on Mount Hira; 3. Evening glow at Seta; 4. Evening bell at Mii temple; 5. Returning sails at Yabase; 6. Clearing winds at Awazu; 7. Night rain on the Karazaki pine; 8. Wild geese alighting at Kataka. The order is not fixed and similar *hakkei* are found relating to other areas. The *mu-tamagawa* (Six crystal rivers) refers to the six rivers, each in a different province, which share the name Tama (jewel, crystal) because of their supposed limpidity. With each was associated a poem and secondary attributes, which are usually present in pictures to designate the river. The rivers, with their attributes are: 1. Kinuta or Toi River (autumn pines and mallets for fulling cloth); 2. Noji River (moonlight and *hagi,* bush-clover) (plate 73); 3. Ide River (*yamabuki,* a yellow rose); 4. Chobu River (bleaching cloth); 5. Koya River (Koya temple or waterfall with pilgrims); 6. Noda River (salt maidens and *chidori,* plovers). The Tokaido and Kisokaido were both roads linking Edo with Kyoto. The Tokaido, 323 miles long, was the shorter route, skirting the coast. The Kisokaido took a longer

95. Hiroshige, *Fuji from Satta Point* from *Thirty-six Views of Fuji,* 1859. *Oban* colour print. Tokyo National Museum.

96. (*Overleaf*) Hokusai, *Fuji seen from Nakahara* from *Thirty-six Views of Fuji,* late 1820s. *Oban* colour print. London, Victoria and Albert Museum.

path through the mountainous interior. Both were divided into sections by villages which acted as resting places and post-stations. Sets of views usually added pictures of both termini thus increasing the stated number of views by two.

Elements of landscape were present, mostly as background scenery, in prints from the time of Moronobu onwards. Illustrated guide-books, *meisho-ki,* were popular but rarely contained pictures of artistic merit. In the 1720s Okumura Masanobu and Shigenaga produced prints of landscape views, rather in the style of the older *yamato-e* album paintings, showing the *Omi hakkei.* These, while interesting, bear little relation to what was to follow. The next important experimental step was the exploration of the possibilities of perspective. Again Okumura Masanobu was in the forefront of this new style known as *Uki-e.* The 1740s and 1750s saw interior views, using perspective, of the theatres (plate 12) and the Yoshiwara by Masanobu, Shigenaga, Moromasa and Kiyotada. The style was given the broader vistas of outdoor themes by Toyoharu in the 1770s and 1780s. Toyoharu (1735–1814), whose designs are still interesting and impressive rather than beautiful, had a central role in the grafting of European ideas to native styles. This was an era when there was a great interest in foreign ideas which were filtering in through prints and books from the Dutch outpost at Nagasaki. Some of Toyoharu's prints are wood-block adaptations of European scenes derived from Dutch prints. The effects of his work were far-reaching and influenced both his direct pupils Toyokuni and Toyohiro (who was later to instruct Hiroshige) and, less directly, the young Hokusai.

Hokusai (1760–1849), during the 1780s and 1790s, was experimenting with any new style which could enable him to wield his fertile brush to greater effect. Apart from his early training in Shunsho's studio, he studied the techniques of the Chinese Ming painters, the academic paintings of the Kano school, *Yamato-e* of the Sumiyoshi school and the Korin style of decorative painting. He was meanwhile designing prints, *surimono* and book illustrations in direct competition with the artists of the popular schools. After Toyoharu revived the *Uki-e* prints, Hokusai, in about 1786, designed a set of perspective prints. By the end of the century the overtly 'Western' influence became more strongly apparent and he produced several sets of landscapes between 1798 and 1802 which had a pronounced European flavour. By 1806 a set of eleven prints depicting scenes from the *Chushingura* shows, in the landscape elements, a degree of fusion in these disparate styles that heralds the mature landscape works for which he is so famous. The epitome of his fully formed style is his set *Thirty-six views of Fuji.* The dating of these prints is not certain. Some say that he began the series as early as 1823 but it is more likely that they came out intermittantly between 1828–33. A publisher's advertisement announces the publication of two of them in 1831. The years 1829–30 saw the vogue for *aizuri-e,* possibly as a result of transiently observed government decrees about highly

97. (*Opposite above*) Hokusai, *Mirror-stand Fuji* from *One Hundred Views of Fuji,* Vol.I, 1834.
Double-page, book-illustration printed in black and two shades of grey. Private Collection.

98. (*Opposite below left*) Hokusai, *Fuji from Ushibori* from *Thirty-six Views of Fuji,* late 1820s. *Oban* colour print. Tokyo National Museum.
A peasant, pouring the water from his rice, disturbs two herons that fly off over the lonely marshes.

99. (*Opposite below right*) Hokusai, *The 'Hanging-cloud' Bridge at Mount Gyodo* from *Novel Views of Famous Bridges in Various Provinces,* late 1820s. *Oban* colour print. London, Victoria and Albert Museum.

100. (*Overleaf left*) Hokusai, *The 'Falling Mist' Waterfall* from *Going the Round of the Waterfalls of the Various Provinces,* c.1830. *Oban* colour print. Kansas City, Nelson-Atkins Gallery.

101. (*Overleaf right*) Hiroshige, *Drum Bridge and Setting-Sun Hill at Meguro* from *One Hundred Views of Edo,* 1857. *Oban* colour print. Roger Nyle Parisious Collection.

102. (*Above*) Hiroshige, *The Temple of Kwannon, Abu-mon in Bingo Province* from *Views of the Sixty-odd Provinces*, 1850. *Oban* colour print. London, British Museum.

103. (*Above right*) Hiroshige, *The 'throwing away the brush' peak at Sakanoshita* from *Fifty-three views of the Tokaido*, c.1833. *Oban* colour print. Tokyo National Museum. The story goes that the celebrated painter Motonobu was so overwhelmed by the beauty of the scene that he threw away his brush in despair.

coloured prints, and several of the set are known in versions coloured almost entirely in shades of blue. It is perhaps not entirely coincidental that these are among the most admired of the series since some of the pigments used for the rest of the prints, a typical yellow-green especially, are not always used in the happiest combinations. Taken overall, however, the series is a fine one. The occasional less successful scene is easily outweighed by the half-dozen masterpieces and the quality of the average designs, which maintain a consistently high level of attractive, artistic invention. The best known and most often re-produced, the *Great Wave, Red Fuji* and *Fuji above the Lightning* are in many ways the least typical. They impress by the majestic grandeur of concept but, where a trace of humanity appears, lost amid the billows at the foot of the *Great Wave*, the men are treated as ciphers, insignificant in comparison to the forces of nature. In the majority of the prints, however, the 'peerless mountain' is present as an integral part of the background to the lives of the Hokusai people who carry on their everyday tasks in the shadow of its beautiful symmetry (plates 96, 107).

In spite of the title *Thirty-six views of Fuji*, there are in fact forty-six prints. It is usually stated that the additional ten prints are found only with a black key-block, the original thirty-six having a blue key-block in their early editions. This is not true since there are, in fact, only seven prints found only with the black key-block: *The Ono paddy-fields; Pilgrims climbing the summit; Dawn at Isawa; Kanaya on the Tokaido; Minobu River; The Senju pleasure quarter; The timber yard at Tatekawa.* (The last-named carries an inscription 'New edition. Thirty-six Fuji completed', presumably indicating that it launches the supplementary ten.) Of the other prints, at least thirteen are found with either blue or black outlines and these seem to bear little relation to the earliness of impression, judged from the wear of the blocks.

At about the time that the *Thirty-six views of Fuji* was being

completed, Hokusai produced two further fine sets, the eleven prints of the *Bridges* (plate 99) and the eight *Waterfalls* (plate 100).

Hokusai was by now over seventy but showed no signs of any slackening off; he was to go on working, especially at book illustration, until his death at the age of eighty-nine in 1849. A rare set of ten *chuban* prints *Oceans of wisdom* showing scenes around the coasts, of about 1833, was followed by an unusual set *Eight views of the Luchu Islands*. These prints are quite unlike his previous work and show a light, dream-like world of islands hovering between sea and sky with touches of deliberately archaic Chinese influence. They are less effective because they lack the human warmth of Hokusai's inimitable Japanese figures. Hokusai then returned to illustrating books. His picture-book *One hundred views of Fuji* (plate 97) published in 1834–5 in three volumes, is a magnificent achievement. His genius never seems to flag as he uses the unifying motif of Fuji to free his flair for inventive composition to rise to ever greater heights. The lack of colour is a positive advantage since it allows his marvellous draughtsmanship to show through.

Hokusai's final important set of prints, to which his landscape skills contributed much, was his series *One hundred poems explained by the nurse* (plate 146). Although over seventy designs are known, only twenty-seven were published in his lifetime. Good as they undoubtedly are, they somehow fall short of his best earlier work and, however high the average quality, there are few that stand out as masterpieces.

Hokusai's great reputation as a landscape-print designer rests largely on the famous sets that he produced in the five years around 1830. The total number of prints contributing to his fame is fewer than a hundred but their quality is high. In this lies part of the great contrast between him and his equally famous younger contemporary Hiroshige.

Hiroshige (1797–1858) first studied under Toyohiro (plate 102). Like Hokusai, however, he broadened his horizons by taking lessons from other schools. He studied Kano painting under Okajima Rinsai,

104. Hokkei, *European ship firing a salute* from *Famous Places in the Provinces*, late 1830s. Large *O-tanzaku* colour print. London, Victoria and Albert Museum. Representing Hizen Province, the extraordinary, archaic galleon, shown in the waters at the mouth of Nagasaki Harbour, was probably derived from pictures of the Portugese traders of the sixteenth century.

Nanga painting under Ooka Umpo and obviously absorbed much from the printed albums of the Shijo school as well as taking an interest in the Western ideas that were coming in. During the 1820s he designed *bijin-ga* in the style of Eisen but, around 1830, he turned to landscape. In 1831 a set of ten *Views of Edo* were well received but his sudden rise to fame occurred after a lengthy trip with a slow-moving ceremonial procession taking gifts from the Shogun in Edo to the Emperor in Kyoto in 1832. They travelled there and back along the Tokaido and Hiroshige filled his sketch-books with views of every village along the route, of Kyoto itself and of nearby Lake Omi. After his return he put these to good use and the next two years saw the publication of several sets of prints that received instant acclaim. Principal among these was his first Tokaido set. The famous highway had often been illustrated but never before had the scenes been so imaginatively and colourfully designed. More importantly, Hiroshige managed to imbue his pictures with the atmosphere of climate and time of day in a manner and with a clarity hitherto unknown. Mists were seen rising in the early morning, rain teemed down or a winter landscape lay silent under deep snow.

Other sets swiftly followed, views of Kyoto and the superb *Eight views of Omi,* each picture redolent of the poem that helped inspire it. The popularity of these sets encouraged the publishers to commission more. There were at least two dozen further sets of Lake Omi and a similar number of sets of Tokaido views, which continued to have a tremendous vogue. He started producing further sets of views of Edo, of which there are a bewildering array. If his scenes of the other places had excited the imagination of the citizens of Edo, his pictures of their home town captured their hearts.

It would be out of place to attempt here to list all of Hiroshige's famous series – he designed more than twelve hundred prints of his beloved Edo alone. Towards the end of his career, however, he produced four sets of upright prints which deserve mention because they are so often encountered and because they show that he was still capable of drawing fresh inspiration from the scenes that he had so often portrayed. These are the *Provinces,* the *Upright Tokaido, Thirty-six views of Fuji* and the *Hundred views of Edo.* The *Provinces,* although occasionally dull, contains many attractive scenes and several splendid prints (plate 102). The *Upright Tokaido* and the *Thirty-six views of Fuji* are less successful although they also contain some fine designs (plate 95). The *Hundred views of Edo,* his last great series, contains some of the least good prints that Hiroshige ever designed but also at least a dozen of his finest masterpieces (plate 101). In many of these prints, part of a prominent foreground object is placed to give an illusion of depth to the remainder of the composition, a device that is sometimes most successful at providing focal interest to an otherwise dull scene (plate 10).

Hiroshige's prints perhaps more than any other's, were reliant on the

105. (*Opposite top*) Hiroshige, *Sailing boats at Arai* from *Fifty-three Views of the Tokaido,* late 1840s. *Chuban* colour print. Private Collection.

106. (*Opposite below*) Hiroshige, *Travellers in the snow at Oi* from *Sixty-nine Stations of the Kisokaido,* late 1830s. *Oban* colour print. London, Victoria and Albert Museum.

107. Eisen, *Returning Boats at Shibaura* from *Eight Views of Edo*, c.1844. *Oban* colour print. Cambridge, Fitzwilliam Museum.

scruples of his printers and publishers. Owing to their popularity some of his sets were reprinted many times, the blocks becoming worn and the colours of the carefully-produced early paintings replaced by fewer, cheaper pigments, shoddily applied (plate 10). Such late impressions, especially when faded and grubby, bear little relation to Hiroshige's original conception but, unfortunately, it is in this state that many of his prints are found to-day. In Japan impressions of Hiroshige prints are graded into nine classes and it is a lucky collector who can find even a medium grade impression to take home to treasure. He is known to have designed over five thousand prints and although probably barely a tenth of these can properly be accounted successes, an artist deserves to be judged by his best work and Hiroshige's best work is superb. There are few artists indeed from whose *oeuvre* one can select so many outstanding designs.

Although Hiroshige was the giant of the mid-nineteenth century landscape, many other artists produced significant work. Hokusai had trained a group of interesting minor artists around 1800. Hokuju (active 1789–1818) designed a sequence of views (plate 125) using a partially assimilated Western style with perspective, shading, billowing clouds in the sky and, sometimes, an odd, almost cubist approach to hills and valleys. Some less well known prints in a similar style were designed by Shinsai (1764?–1820), who is otherwise mainly noted for his *surimono*. Hokkei (1780–1850) designed a small number of good landscape prints and produced one important set in *yoko-e o-tanzaku* format (plate 104). Thirteen of these are known and they show a verve and imagination often lacking in other topographical prints of the time. His pupil Gakutei (1786?–1868) moved from Edo to Osaka and is acclaimed for a set of six *oban* prints of Mount Tempo, Osaka, originally published as

an album in 1834 (plate 101). These magnificent designs, glowing with colour, can easily stand against the work of their artistic progenitor, Hokusai. It is a pity that Gakutei did not do more.

Eisen's landscapes came out during the 1830s, the hey-day of Hokusai and Hiroshige. His style was influenced by both, yet shows distinct individuality. The twenty-four prints that he contributed to the Kisokaido set in collaboration with Hiroshige between 1835 and 1837 fail to reach the highest standards of Hiroshige's best designs but easily hold their own with the rest. His foreground figures are well drawn and their everyday activities are cleverly observed. When the series was completed, probably in the early 1840s, there was a reissue of the entire set. Eisen's designs had the signature removed, presumably in an attempt to pass off the whole as the work of the popular Hiroshige. He also designed several *oban* sets of views of Edo. One of the most successful is a set of *Eight views* (plate 107). In about 1844 he produced a fine set of eight upright prints *Famous views in the Nikko Mountains*, showing the waterfalls for which the area is famous.

The students of Toyokuni made surprisingly little effort to compete in the field of landscape. Toyokuni himself produced several dozen *Uki-e* prints, many of them landscapes but none of them of great merit. Of his many pupils, Kunitora, Kuninaga (d.1829), Kuniyasu and Kuninao did occasional prints in this field but, apart from a certain fascination at those rare prints by Kuninaga and Kunitora which were cribbed directly from European engravings (views of the Colossus of Rhodes were especially popular!), their prints were mostly artistically mundane or inept. Plate 108 by Kunitora illustrates a better and distinctive style which had a vogue about 1820, where soft colours, much use of blind printing and archaic conventions (such as the

108. Kunitora, *Sunrise at Futami*, c.1820. *Oban* colour print. Private Collection. The 'Wedded Rocks' at Futami beach, joined by straw ropes, form an important Shinto shrine. They represent Izanagi and Izanami, the mythological creators of Japan. The view of them with the sun rising over Ise Bay is especially famous.

109. Hiroshige II, *The harbour of Muronotsu, Harima Province, in snow* from *One Hundred Views of the Provinces*, 1859. *Oban* colour print. Private Collection.

formalized bands of clouds) predominate. The other main exponent of such prints was Kashosai Shunsen.

Toyokuni II (Toyoshige) surprises everyone by one set of landscapes, unlike anything else that he did, the *Eight views of famous places,* which stand out among the other topographical prints of the mid-1830s by owing little to either Hiroshige or Hokusai. The set contains several excellent designs (plate 94). No other comparable work by him is known and it may be that he died (in 1835) before he had time to follow them up.

Kunisada designed a few landscapes in the 1830s. Several of these were based on pictures in Bumpo's *Ehon sansui gafu* of 1824. His *Landscape in mist* stands out as exceptional but his prints in this genre obviously failed to find favour and he reverted to actor prints and *bijin-ga,* where his reputation had been made.

Kuniyoshi's landscape prints are rightly regarded highly. His two sets of views of Edo from the early 1830s, the five prints titled *Toto* and the ten *Toto meisho* contain some of his most admired work. The 'Westernized' clouds in the sky, the sometimes eerie effects of his choice of vantage point and the almost invariable prominence of the foreground figures are characteristic. These are not landscape views with figures so much as pictures of the local inhabitants, marvellously caught in their normal settings. A set of twelve Tokaido views, each showing a vista of several stations, came out the year after Hiroshige completed his first Tokaido series. Many of the devices of composition owe much to Hiroshige – the carefully graded band of colour at the top of a plain sky, distant mountains printed without outline, and a skilful use of colour to break up successive ranges of hills. Kuniyoshi had by now so assimilated the techniques of perspective that he was able to give the successful illusion of depth to his landscapes without inducing the 'vanishing rails' optical effect of the *Uki-e* or the slightly awkward appearances sometimes seen in the prints of Kunitora or Hokuju. None of this set manages to convey that sense of atmosphere that marks Hiroshige's finest efforts but they remain interesting and pleasing prints nonetheless. In the five prints from the unfinished set of *Thirty-six views of Fuji,* the foreground action again tends to take the attention away from the scenery. Plate 93 is typical, the symmetry of Fuji in the distance counterpointed by the conflicting curves of the boats, fishing nets and sails of the jostling craft in Edo Bay.

Some of Kuniyoshi's most famous 'landscapes' are the subsidiary, if important, settings for the intended subject of the prints. This comes over most clearly in some of his celebrated set depicting scenes from the life of the Buddhist saint Nichiren and in the series *Twenty-four Paragons of Filial Piety.* The moral fables relating to the paragons were of foreign (albeit Chinese) origin and Kuniyoshi took the opportunity to parade his grasp of 'foreign' design even to the extent of lifting the scene of one of the most famous from the set (plate 126) from an unidentified

European print.

When Hiroshige died in 1858, his pupil Shigenobu married his daughter and assumed his name, becoming known as Hiroshige II (1826–69). It is not known how much he was involved in such sets as the *Thirty-six views of Fuji* or the *Upright Tokaido*, although there is clear evidence that some of the *Hundred views of Edo* were his work. Nor is it clear how much of his subsequent output over the next four or five years was reliant on sketches and preliminary designs left by his master, although Strange quotes the preface to the eighth volume of an illustrated book *Edo miyage* (1861): 'It is now a memorial of him (Hiroshige I) since he is dead, but from sketches left behind are these views reproduced'. Hiroshige II is best known for his series *One hundred views of famous places in the Provinces* (plate 110). Eighty-one prints are known from the uncompleted series issued between 1859–64. Many of these are excellent compositions and, when well printed, are fully equal to the later work assigned to Hiroshige I. Throughout the early 1860s he produced several sets of Edo views and he was also designing *Yokohama-e* in single-sheets and triptychs (see page 155). In September 1865 he divorced his wife and moved to Yokohama where he continued to work using the name Ryushu (Rissho). The Hiroshige name was continued by a young artist Shigemasa, who became Hiroshige III. He produced prints of interest rather than beauty, showing the modernization of Japan after the restoration of the monarchy. His prints and triptychs were issued between 1868–84 and document the coming of the railways, trams and brick-built buildings.

Other Hiroshige followers include Hirokage (active 1855–65), Fusatane (active 1849–70) and Sadanobu (1809–79), who worked in Osaka and produced his own version of many of Hiroshige's designs, not wholly unsuccessfully.

Many of the pupils of Kuniyoshi and Kunisada worked mainly on the *Yokohama-e* but Kyosai, the famous painter, had studied with Kuniyoshi as a boy and designed an upright set of Tokaido views in 1866 using the signature Chikamaro.

The 1880s saw a resurgence of prints of landscape scenes when the impact of the new arts of photography and Western realistic painting began to influence the Japanese prints. Kiyochika was outstanding and, although many of his prints suffer from unfortunate colour schemes, his talent as an artist shows through and renders many of his designs important aesthetically rather than just as pictorial reporting. Perhaps because of the colouring, many of his best prints are night scenes. He worked from the mid-1870s to the turn of the century but his best prints date from the period 1876–81. His pupil Yasuji (1864–89) showed great promise and designed some excellent landscapes in the early 1880s but unfortunately he died young. In somewhat the same style Ryuson (active 1880–90) specialized in moonlit night scenes that are often strikingly effective.

7
Studies of Nature

Kacho-ga, pictures of birds and flowers, were one of the three traditional subjects of Chinese painting. The Chinese-inspired academic schools of painting in Japan and the Nanga and Shijo artists worked extensively in this field but the commercial print artists in Edo, with a few notable exceptions, rarely specialized in the subject. Whether birds, animals or plants occur as the main subject of a print or only as an incidental part, they will often be found to have an emblematic significance. The closest analogy in Western tradition would be the incidence on Christmas cards of mistletoe, holly, Christmas trees and robins perched on snow-covered logs. In Japan every season had its festivals, every month its special flowers and delicacies and the hours and years were marked by an animal from the zodiac. In addition, the conventions of the art of poetry, to which every cultured Japanese aspired, forged links between the contemplation of nature and human emotion to an extent that it is rare to find a picture containing a flower or animal where some secondary allusion is not intended. There are some conventional groups of flowers: the 'Three Friends', pine, bamboo and plum blossom; 'Four Noble Plants', orchid, bamboo, plum and chrysanthemum. *Surimono* often show emblems of the New Year, especially young pine trees and bamboo. The crane, deer and tortoise suggest longevity.

As mentioned above, the printed albums of the Classical schools frequently depict birds and flowers (plates 111, 132). These beautiful, impressionistic prints are rarely found as single-sheets although occasional *surimono* or dismounted pages from albums are encountered.

Although they form but a small proportion of the Edo broadsheets, *kacho-ga* can be found at most periods. In the early days Kiyomasu, Shigenaga and others designed some large prints of birds, mostly the hawk-eagle and other birds of prey. In 1720 Ooka Shumboku published his *Ehon Takagami,* a painting manual, and Okumura Masanobu designed several prints of birds based on designs taken from it. Shigenaga's *hosoban* print of pheasants (plate 113) dates from a little later. With the coming of colour printing Koryusai stands out as the artist of several dozen fine *kacho-ga,* mostly in *chuban* size (plate 110) but also as pillar prints and *surimono* (plate 114). His name is also associated with some very rare *kakemono-e* prints of birds in *ichizuri-e* style, designed to imitate the ancient Chinese stone-rubbings.

110. Koryusai, *Crane and Bamboo,* mid-1770s. *Chuban* colour print. Chicago, Art Institute of Chicago.
The poem reads:—
'His acrobatic dexterity probably learned from a *sennin,* the crane picking his feed while perched on a single bamboo pole'.

104

Between 1787 and 1791 Utamaro was the artist of a remarkable sequence of albums. The *Insect Book*, (plate 127) published in 1787, contains fifteen double-page illustrations of insects or reptiles amid flowers or fruits. The *Shell Book* came out two or three years later and, in 1791, the *Bird Book* completed the trilogy. Each provided illustrations to the effusions of members of poetry clubs, who had contributed humorous verses, *kyoka*. The only comparable work of this era was the album by Kitao Masayoshi (1764–1824), *A mirror of birds and flowers* (plate 136) of 1789, which may have been based on an album of Chinese paintings. This contains twelve *oban* prints of birds.

Many of the best *kacho-ga*, however, stem from the nineteenth century. Hokusai produced two famous sets, which have become known as the 'large' and 'small' flowers because of their format. The 'large flowers' of about 1830 are a series of ten *oban* sheets of flowers, most of them also incorporating an insect, finely printed on a plainly coloured ground. They are marvellously designed with all of Hokusai's adept draughtsmanship and skilful composition. The colour harmonies are sometimes less fortunate and I have often felt a sense of slight disappointment on seeing 'in the flesh' some of these that I have admired so much in black and white reproduction (plate 116). They seem to be very rare. Prints from another *oban* set of *kacho-ga* with Hokusai signatures have usually been attributed to his pupil Taito II (active 1810–53) since the same designs appear in an illustrated book *Kacho-gaden* (1848–9) by Taito II, but Lane has recently suggested that they are Meiji prints based on the earlier designs.

The 'small flowers' of about 1832 are delightful. Each print carefully names the birds and flowers shown and is accompanied by a poem in the Chinese style (plate 117). These ten *chuban* prints are even rarer than the 'large flowers' in spite of apparently going into at least three editions. Hokusai also designed a set of *chuban aizuri-e* prints of birds, a

114. (*Above*) Koryusai, *Chrysanthemums*, c.1780. Large colour-printed *surimono* 6¾ × 18¾ in (16.8 × 47.3 cm). Chicago, Art Institute of Chicago.
Probably issued for the 'Chrysanthemum Festival', held every year on the ninth day of the ninth month.

111. (*Opposite above*) Taki Katei (1830–1901), *Bamboos*, 1894. Album plate printed in shades of grey and black, from *Tanjo Ippan* (Models for Painting). Private Collection.
From an instructional album by one of the most skilful and meticulous painters working in the Chinese style.

112. (*Opposite below left*) Shumman, *Owl on magnolia branch*, c.1800. Square *surimono*, 7¼ × 7 in (18.4 × 17.8 cm). London, Victoria and Albert Museum.

113. (*Opposite below right*) Shigenaga, *Silver pheasants and waterfall*, mid-1720s. *Hosoban*, hand-coloured *beni-e*. Manchester, Whitworth Art Gallery.

115. (*Above*) Hokusai, *Two cranes on a snowy pine*, c.1833. *Naga-ban* colour print. Minneapolis, Minneapolis Institute of Art (Gale Collection).

116. (*Opposite above*) Hokusai, *Tiger lilies*, c.1830. *Oban* colour print. Tokyo National Museum.

117. (*Opposite below left*) Hokusai, *Kingfisher, iris and pinks*, c.1832. *Chuban* colour print. London, Victoria and Albert Museum.
The Chinese poem has been translated: 'Looking forward and backward as he perches, he seems like a moving jewel of deep blue and green'. (Waley.)

118. (*Opposite below right*) Hiroshige, *Kingfisher and Hydrangea*, early 1830s. *O-tanzaku* colour print. Tokyo National Museum.

group of five *naga-ban* prints (plate 115) and several sets of *surimono* featuring birds and flowers (plate 118).

At about the same time, in the early 1830s, Hiroshige was beginning to produce his typical *kacho-ga*. These have a quite different style, derived in part from his earlier studies under a tutor of the Shijo school. They were usually produced in the various sizes of the *tanzaku* (poetry paper) format and they mostly carry apt poems by contemporary poets. There are twenty-five of the larger *O-tanzaku* prints, most of them first published by Jakurindo and later reissued by Kikakudo, and fifty-seven *chu-tanzaku* prints likewise put out originally by Yamaguchi and reissued by Fujioka. A comparison of the two treatments of the kingfisher by Hokusai (plate 117) and Hiroshige (plate 118) shows clearly their differences in approach. Hokusai, illustrating a poem about a kingfisher, uses his consummate draughtsmanship to produce a meticulously detailed picture (although not entirely true to life – the iris and the pinks would not be found blooming together). Hiroshige, using a poem about a hydrangea, introduces a kingfisher to call to mind the 'smell of water', mentioned in the poem. He affects a softer, more impressionistic style. Hokusai's best designs are very beautiful, Hiroshige's are very pretty.

Hiroshige also designed several sets of pictures of fishes in both *oban* and *chuban* format and some fan prints. The two sets of *oban* prints, ten in each, are collectively known as the 'large fishes'. Each has a *kyoka* poem. The first set was published by Eijudo in the early 1830s, probably as a private commission for a poetry club and the second by Yamasho about ten years later. They were subsequently republished together in album form and seem to have been often reissued as it is not uncommon to find quite worn impressions with evidence of recut blocks. The presence of touches of mica on some of these prints is, of itself, no guide to the edition, as this can be found on quite late impressions.

Kuniyoshi was skilled at drawing animals and these often make incidental appearances in his prints. He is noted for his particular affection for cats. His only formal series of *kacho-ga* is found in a very rare and impressive set of *tanzaku* prints of aquatic subjects.

Eisen, who is more usually associated with his highly successful pictures of popular beauties and landscapes, is less well known as a designer of *kacho-ga* but his work in this field shows a sensitive artistic talent and can well stand comparison with his more famous contemporaries. He usually signs such work with his *go*, Keisei (plate 131). He is known to have been interested in Chinese paintings and his masterly study of bamboos against the full moon, done in shades of blue, is as striking as it is unexpected, using, as it does, a style of art far removed from the usual Edo broadsheets (plate 121).

Sugakudo, a pupil of Hiroshige, is known for two sets of *oban* prints, *Exact Representations of Forty-eight Hawks* (i.e. birds) of 1858, reissued as

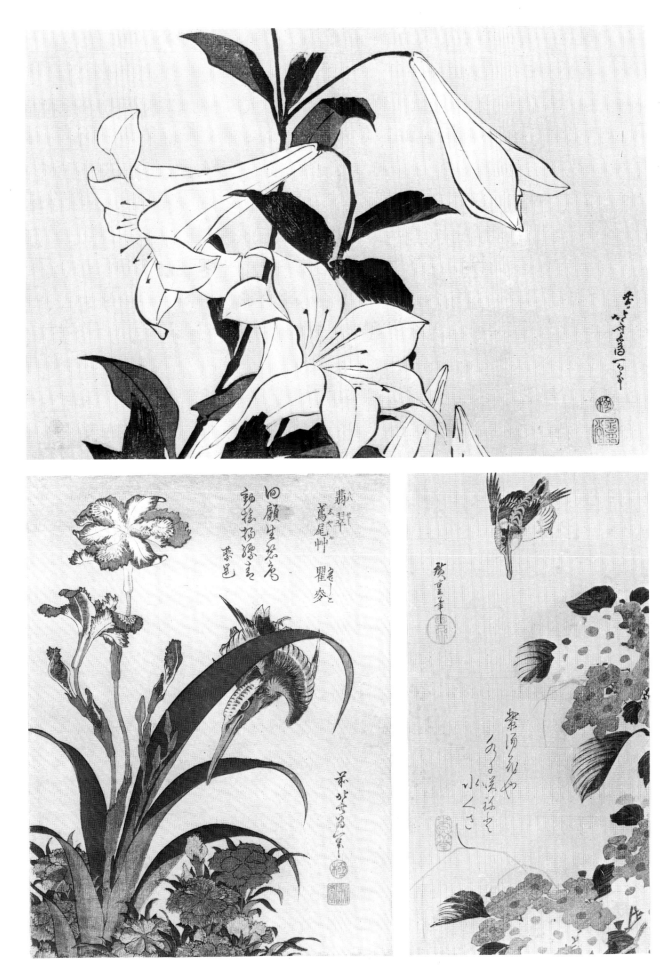

119. Hiroshige, *Peacock on aronia branch*, c.1830. *Chuban* colour print. Tokyo National Museum.

120. Kyosai, *Two crows on a flowering plum in winter*, c.1870. *Kakemono-e* colour print. Private Collection. The printer and engraver have carefully emulated the effect of the artist's brush strokes rather than producing the more usual outline print enclosing flat colour.

雨洗娟ゝ
淨風吹
細ゝ香
岡南
こ

121. Eisen, *Bamboo and moon*, c.1840.
Oban colour print, *aizuri-e*. Manchester,
Whitworth Art Gallery.
The poem reads:—
'The rain cleanses so beautifully, a soft
breeze breathes a delicate scent.'

an album the following year, with a supplement in 1860, and *Birds and Flowers of the Four Seasons* of 1861. These are attractive designs characterized by fine printing and embossing but with a rather unfortunate bright yellow border, which is often trimmed off. It has been suggested that Sugakudo was a pseudonym used by Tazaki Soun (1815–98), a *nanga* painter.

Kyosai (1831–89), who was renowned for his paintings of birds, is notable for a small number of superb prints of crows (plate 120). These were printed in the 1870s mainly in finely gradated monochrome with occasional touches of colour. Kono Bairei (1844–95), a painter and co-founder of an important art school in Kyoto in 1880, is noted for his illustrated books. Zeshin (1807–91), the lacquer master, was also an accomplished painter, grafting his own eclectic, decorative style on to his formal training in the Shijo manner under Nanrei and Toyohiko. His broad, artistic talents also led him to design prints (plate 184) and *surimono*. He was adept at using the cut-off at the borders of his designs to enhance the effect of his pictures. Most often encountered is a series of small prints titled (on the original wrapper) *Hana kurabe* published by Haibara between 1875 and 1890. A pirated edition, not quite so finely printed, was issued by Nishioka about 1890 and these sometimes carry the false signatures of other artists. Other important albums of *kacho-ga* were produced in the 1880s by Imao Keinen (1845–1924) and Watanabe Seitei (1851–1918).

嶋村彈正高則

8
Literature and Legend

Japan is rich in folklore and historical and fictional legends. These, and themes from classical literature, appear in many guises in the prints. They may be found as analogues or parodies (*mitate*) to link sets, as scenes from plots in *kabuki* prints or as straight representations of the subjects. A knowledge of the stories illustrated in the prints adds considerably to their interest and large volumes have been compiled detailing such myths and legends. This chapter can do no more than mention some of the most important.

Figures from the native Shinto creation myths or the slightly later, Chinese derived, Buddhist and Taoist legends are sometimes seen. Often depicted are the seven lucky gods: Hotei with his huge belly and sack (plate 123); Jurojin with his emblems of longevity; Fukurojin with his high domed head; Bishamon armed with a spear; Daikoku, the god of wealth, with a bale of rice and a cheerful grin; Ebisu with his fish; and Benten, the sea goddess. These may be shown either alone or sailing in the *takarabune,* the treasure ship. To sleep with a picture of this ship under the pillow at the New Year was supposed to ensure lucky dreams. Daruma, the old sage who had brought Zen Buddhism from India to China, is shown with his oddly staring eyes, having cut off his eyelids to avoid falling asleep during meditation. Shoki, the demon queller, dressed as a T'ang official with a Chinese sword (plate 128) is often shown chasing one of the varieties of small devils. There were three main classes of such demons or goblins: *oni,* with horns and three digits (plate 163); *tengu,* either winged and birdlike or humanoid with long noses; and *kappa,* water demons with scaley skins and a typical indentation of the skull. Mythical beasts also abounded. Dragons (plate 150) were probably the most impressive but *kirin,* a lucky unicorn, *shishi,* highly modified lions or the *Ho-o* bird (plate 124), a sort of phoenix, may also be met. Less exotic animals may take on magical properties or emblematic significance. Foxes and badgers can assume human shape; mandarin ducks signify marital fidelity; cranes, tortoises and stags are symbols of longevity; and carp signify endurance in adversity and are often shown in connection with the Boy's Festival, a celebration on the fifth day of the fifth month.

The twenty-four Chinese fables about paragons of filial piety were well known (plates 41, 126, 147). Such stories found favour in Japan, where duty and loyalty, both in the family and to the state, were exalted

122. Kuniyoshi, *Shimamura Danjo Takanori*, c.1843. *Oban* colour print. Private Collection.
Takanori, a warrior in the civil wars of the sixteenth century, drowned himself when his army was defeated at Amagaseki in 1532. The crabs in that district are said to have since borne marks in his likeness on their shells.

123. Yoshitoshi, *Hotei and the moon of enlightenment* from *One Hundred Views of the Moon*, 1888. *Oban* colour print. Private Collection.
Hotei, the happy God of felicity and contentment, was the most popular of the Seven Lucky Gods (page 111). He is shown leaning back on his bag of treasures, pointing at the moon in a state of ecstatic enlightenment.

ideals.

The world of the courtly poetry and literature of the ninth and tenth centuries comes into the prints through the *Tales of Ise,* the life of Ono no Komachi, the *Tale of Genji* and the anthologies of classical poetry. The *Ise monogatari,* the tales of Ise, consist of over two hundred poems, mostly those of Ariwara Narihira (825–880) and the replies of the ladies to whom he addressed his amorous verses, loosely linked by fictional prose settings. The fullest treatment of these in the prints was in Shunsho's two sets of about 1770, totalling forty-eight prints.

Ono no Komachi, the only woman among the 'six poetic geniuses' of the ninth century, was reputed to have been beautiful, skilful at repartee, passionate yet often hard-hearted and cruel to her innumerable lovers. Legends about her life and loves became codified in the *Seven Komachi* stories, a series of *noh* plays of the fourteenth century. These are often parodied in the prints. The episodes are: 1. *Soshi arai,* Komachi washing the fresh ink from a book of poetry after she is accused of plagiarism (plate 157); 2. *Sekidera,* the aged and impoverished poetess by a thatched hut talking to a priest and children during the Tanabata festival; 3. *Kiyomizu,* talking to a priest at the Kiyomizu temple, famous for its flowering cherries (plate 86); 4. *Kayoi,* the nobleman Fukakusa, who courted her outside her gate for one hundred nights only to die of cold on the final night (plate 31); 5. *Amagoi,* during a drought she composed a poem successfully invoking rain; 6. *Omu* or 'parrot', because she returned a poem from the Emperor altering only one syllable; 7. *Sotoba,* Komachi sitting on a holy Buddhist monument worsts in argument the priests, who remonstrate with her.

The fifty-four chapters of the *Tale of Genji,* the long tenth century novel about the romantic life of Prince Genji, was also often parodied and illustrated (plates 6, 124). The episode is often named or indicated by the distinctive *Genji-mon,* a motif of five vertical bars variously joined at the top.

Series of prints may be found linked to the 'six poets', the 'thirty-six poets' and the 'one hundred poets'. The last was a well known sequence of poets and poems made popular by a game in which cards bearing the pictures of each of the poets had to be matched with the cards bearing their poems. Famous print series of the 'hundred poets' were produced by Kuniyoshi (plate 11) and Hokusai (plate 146).

The *Heike monogatari,* a compilation of tales, part historical, part legendary, describing the events of the civil wars of the twelfth century, was a fruitful source of subjects for *kabuki* plays and *musha-e,* warrior pictures. The two clans, the Taira (Heike) and the Minamoto, strove bloodily for overall control of Japan for more than a generation. Taira Kiyomori (plate 150) held power until his death but heroes of the Minamoto, Yoritomo, Yoshinaka and Yoshitsune, then defeated the Taira in a succession of famous battles and finally annihilated them at the sea battle of Dan-no-ura. Meanwhile dissent in the Minamoto camp

led to internicine strife and first Yoshinaka was killed at the battle of Uji River by Yoritomo's forces under Yoshitsune and finally Yoshitsune himself was pursued to his death by Yoritomo, who ended with ultimate control. The exploits of the young, brilliant general Yoshitsune and his versatile, strong-arm henchman Benkei, incorporating adventure, loyalty, bravery and eventual tragedy, made him into a popular, Robin Hood-type hero. Yoshitsune's uncle Tametomo, another semi-legendary hero, was a powerful archer and is seen undergoing many improbable adventures. He is often shown sinking a Taira ship with a single arrow.

Yoritomo also features in the *Soga-monogatari,* the story of the Soga brothers, Juro and Goro. The brothers were only infants when their father was murdered by Kudo Suketsune (plate 55), who rose to become a powerful *daimyo* and advisor to Yoritomo. Eighteen years after the murder, the avenging brothers fought their way into a heavily guarded hunting camp and slew Suketsune. Juro was killed in the ensuing mêlée and Goro was captured and later executed. The story was popular in the *kabuki* and one of the plays of the 'Soga world' would always be performed at the New Year. The brothers can often be identified by the patterns of butterflies (Goro) and plovers (Juro) on their robes. The plays often deal with the problems that beset their preparations for revenge and involve Juro's mistress, Tora-gozen, and Asahina Saburo, famous for his feats of strength (plates 15, 29).

The other famous story of loyalty and revenge is the *Chushingura,* the story of the forty-seven *ronin* (masterless samurai). In 1701 Asano, Lord of Ako, during a quarrel with a high official, Kira Kozuke, struck at him with his sword within the precincts of the Shogun's palace. Asano only wounded his adversary but his punishment was death by suicide (*seppuku*), while his heirs were dispossessed of land and his retainers left without income or master. Forty-seven of the latter resolved to avenge their master's death. After two years during which they schemed and dissembled, they gathered secretly and attacked the nobleman's fortified home, slew his bodyguards and killed him. All forty-seven gave themselves up and were subsequently condemned to death but, as a concession, were allowed to commit *seppuku*. This evocation of supreme loyalty fired the imagination of the Japanese and

124. Toyokuni III (Kunisada), *Self portrait of the artist* representing 'painting' from *Genji Parallels of the Four Accomplishments,* 1866. Colour-printed *oban* triptych. Private Collection.
The scene is the famous 'Phoenix Hall' of the Choji-ya (House of the Clove) in the *Yoshiwara.* Kunisada, identified by his *toshidama* motif on his sleeve, is shown superintending the refurbishing of the huge painting of a *Ho-o* bird on the wall. The design closely mimics a similar self-portrait by Utamaro of sixty years before. The triptych is signed 'The seventy-nine year old Toyokuni' but, like several others with this signature, the date seal shows that it was published posthumously.

125. (*Overleaf above left*) Hokuju, *Monkey Bridge in Koshu Province,* c.1815. *Oban* colour print. London, Victoria and Albert Museum.
The 'Monkey' Bridge, spanning a deep gorge, is so-called because the original, rickety, plank bridge was such that it was said that only an agile monkey would have been expected to venture across it.

126. (*Overleaf below left*) Kuniyoshi, *Sosan returning to his mother* from *Twenty-four Paragons of Filial Piety,* c.1840. *Oban* colour print. Private Collection.
Sosan's mother, vexed by his absence, bit her finger. Sosan, cutting wood in the forest, felt an overwhelming compulsion to return and is seen hurrying home across the bridge.

127. (*Overleaf right*) Utamaro, *Rice locust, red dragon-fly, pinks and Chinese bell flowers,* 1788. Double-page, colour-printed book illustration from Vol. 2 of *A Picture Book of Selected Insects*. London, British Museum.

128. (*Above*) Kiyomasu, *Shoki the demon queller*, c.1714. *Kakemono-e* hand-coloured *tan-e*. Chicago, Art Institute of Chicago.

129. (*Above right*) Shunei, *Asahina attempting to restrain Soga no Goro*, c.1800. *Chuban* colour print. Manchester, Whitworth Art Gallery.
Asahina, the legendary strong man, attempts to stop Goro from leaving by grabbing the tightly woven lappet of his armour. Goro, however, no weakling himself, walks away leaving Asahina clenching the part that he held.

130. (*Opposite*) Kuniyoshi, *Nozarashi Satosuke* from *Kuniyoshi's Types of Wayward Young Men*, c.1845. Private Collection.
Kuniyoshi's ingenious arrangement of cats to make up the design of skulls on the cloak is typical.

dramatized versions of these events were on the stage within three years. The episodes depicted in the prints mostly show scenes from the eleven act play *Kanahedon Chushingura*, staged every December. Because of laws relating to plays about contemporary events, the dates, localities and names were changed and, for the purpose of the drama, many fictional incidents were incorporated. Often shown is the final night attack, when each of the loyal *ronin* is shown wearing a distinctive costume of alternating black and white triangles.

Heroic figures occur frequently in the prints and even if the *kabuki* characters be excluded, as being but melodramatic adaptations, there remain *musha-e* published from the earliest times until the twentieth century. Several single-sheet *oban* prints of warriors by anonymous artists during the 1660s are among the first non-erotic prints still extant. Prints of Shoki the demon-queller (plate 128) were pasted on to doors as talismans from at least 1690 and many of the popular artists of the eighteenth and nineteenth centuries produced versions. They are often shown displayed at the time of the Boy's Festival. Okumura Masanobu designed albums showing the exploits of Japanese heroes, pictures of the lucky gods and parodies of *sennin* (Taoist immortals). During the eighteenth century, however, *musha-e* formed but a tiny proportion of the print subjects. Before full-colour, the Torii artists and Shigenaga designed a few and, later, Shunsho and his school (plate 128), Masayoshi and Toyoharu tried their hands but, during the whole of this period and well into the early nineteenth

131. (*Left*) Eisen, *Sparrows and Camellia*, c.1820. *Kakemono-e* colour print. London, Victoria and Albert Museum.

132. (*Opposite*) Nangaku (1763–1813), *Ripe Persimmons*, c.1810. Colour-printed, large album plate. London, Victoria and Albert Museum.
Nangaku studied under Maruyama Okyo in Kyoto. A notable painter and teacher himself, he was the first to introduce the Maruyama style to Edo in the early nineteenth century.

133. (*Opposite above*) Kiyochika, *The village headman Sogoro pleading with the old ferryman, Jimbei*, 1884. Colour-printed *oban* triptych. Private Collection. Sogoro travelled to the capital to petition the *shogun* to remit the excessive taxes levied by a grasping noble. The taxes were remitted but the noble had Sogoro and his family cruelly put to death. The story of the subsequent haunting by the vengeful spirit of Sogoro is a favourite ghost story.

134. (*Opposite below left*) Yoshitoshi, *The actor Bando Hikosaburo V as Kagekiyo* from *Tales of Contemporary Personalities*, 1887. *Oban* colour print. Private Collection. Kagekiyo was one of the few survivors from the Taira forces when they were overwhelmingly defeated at the sea-battle of Dan-no-ura in the twelfth century. Legend and history differ about his subsequent fate. Legend states that he escaped and after an unsuccessful attempt on the life of Yoritomo, put out his own eyes to avoid seeing his enemies triumph. History suggests that he was captured after the battle and died from refusal to take food in captivity.

135. (*Opposite below right*) Kunisada, *The actor Matsumoto Koshiro V as Nikki Danjo*, c.1812. *Oban* colour print. Private Collection. Nikki Danjo is a villainous character in the play *Meiboku Sendai Hagi* ('The Disputed Succession'). He has magical powers and is shown here appearing in a cloud of smoke.

century, the main vehicle for such subjects was the illustrated book. The blood-thirsty, complicated episodes of the novels written by Bakin (1767–1848) became incredibly successful in the first quarter of the nineteenth century. He wrote popular versions of the *Heike Monogatari*, rehashed many of the old Japanese legends, especially those which were fantastical, involving magic and phantoms. He wove fictional tales about impossible heroes (e.g. *Hakkenden*, the violent lives of the eight dog-heroes, offspring of a nobleman's daughter and a dog) and adapted from the Chinese the romance concerning the lives of a ferocious band of brigands, the *Suikoden*.

Many of these texts were illustrated by Hokusai, whose stalwart warriors, eerie ghosts and shrinking maidens rescued from horribly bewhiskered Chinese villains, well matched the stories. These books must have taken up much of Hokusai's time during this period. They were issued in many small volumes, an episode at a time. The *Hakkenden*, for example, came out in one hundred and six volumes and *Suikoden* (started by Bakin, completed by Ranzan but illustrated throughout by Hokusai) filled ninety volumes issued between 1807 and 1828. Surprisingly Hokusai designed few *musha-e* prints, although a set of five was published, probably in about 1829 (plate 8). During the 1810s Shuntei (1770–1820), a pupil of Shunei, had designed some warrior prints but they lacked the verve needed for success. It was not until the advent of Kuniyoshi that the style of warrior print that was to flourish for the rest of the century became established. Prints of heroes and heroines, triptychs of famous battles and legendary monsters vanquished: these were Kuniyoshi's forte. He first made his mark with a long series of the heroes of the *Suikoden* published between 1827 and 1830. This was about the time that Hokusai was completing the book edition in black and white but Kuniyoshi drew his own style of warrior, colourful and exuberant, the action filling an *oban* sheet (plate 143). The set was wildly successful and a *Suikoden* craze ensued with Kuniyoshi and others using the popular title on sets which seem to bear little relation to the Chinese story. A fine set of *surimono* showing women in fashionable kimonos was titled *Suikoden of women's customs*. More on the lines of the original set, a series of Japanese heroes, *800 Suikoden of our country* (plate 61) came out intermittantly during the 1830s. Kuniyoshi had found his metier and, although he could and did produce fine work in other fields, he explored the whole realm of Japan's rich and colourful history in set after set of prints. Many of these carry extensive explanatory text and they may, in part, have taken on the role previously filled by the picture books. Not that all his forays into Japan's past were restricted to pictures of armed warriors. In a similar, but gentler vein, he showed brave and loyal heroines and his *One hundred poems by one hundred poets* of about 1840 adopted a refined style perfectly suited to his subject (plate 10). Kuniyoshi was a master of many facets but in the fields of legend and history he reigns supreme.

鶍
禽

136. (*Above*) Kitao Masayoshi, *Warbler and Peonies*, 1789. Colour-printed album plate from *A Mirror of Birds and Flowers*. London, British Museum.

137. (*Opposite*) Kuniyoshi, *Oniwaka-maru fighting a giant carp*, c.1830. *Oban* colour print. Private Collection.
Oniwaka-maru, 'young devil child' was a nickname of the young Benkei who later became the faithful retainer of Yoshitsune. He is shown fighting a gigantic carp by the waterfall of Bishamon ga taki. The carp is said to have devoured Benkei's mother who had fallen into the river.

122

His is the work that forms the yardstick against which all others are judged.

Hiroshige had designed some heroic diptychs in about 1820, rather in the style of Shuntei, but these seem to have met with little success. Later, after he was established and secure, he produced several sets on heroic themes; the *Biography of Yoshitsune*; a *Chushingura* set in about 1835; the *Soga Brothers* and several heroic triptychs in the mid-1840s; and an interesting set of Genji illustrations in Tosa style in 1852. During the 1840s he collaborated with Kuniyoshi and Kunisada in several sets of prints which evaded the restrictions on publishing actor prints by purporting to show legendary scenes.

Kunisada, although he mostly concentrated on actor prints and *bijin-ga*, is noted for a few rare *musha-e*. At about the time of Kuniyoshi's success with the *Suikoden*, Kunisada designed a set of Chinese warriors *Kanso Gunden, War stories of Han and Ch'u* (China) published by Eijudo. These were followed by an untitled set of Japanese warriors, their names set in an irregular white cartouche against a dark ground (plate 142), published by Daikoku-ya. These seem to have been special commissions. The printing is especially fine and the signature is prefixed *motome ni ojite* 'by special request'. The triptych of the three generals of Han (plate 5) dates from about the same time. A little later, about 1834–5, a further set of *musha-e* was put out by Morita-ya (plate 145).

Kuniyoshi's predilection for heroic triptychs of battling warriors was continued by some of his many pupils. Most notable were Yoshitoshi,

Yoshitsuya (1822–66), Yoshitora, Yoshifusa (active 1837–60), Yoshikazu and Yoshitaki (1841–99). Fresh impetus for such prints came from the bloody events of the 1860s. A series of minor civil wars, which led finally to the defeat of the *Shogun's* forces and the restoration of the monarchy, were compounded by the anti-foreigner campaigns, assassinations and reprisals by the Western powers. These events were rarely depicted directly in the prints owing to the censorship laws. But triptychs showing armed clashes, ostensibly from the histories of the inter-clan strife of medieval Japan and pictures of valiant Japanese heroes fighting off boat-loads of Korean invaders (appearing to refer to events of the sixteenth century) suddenly took on greater relevance.

With the coming of peace in 1868 these prints tended to die out. Yoshitoshi, who seems to have had a macabre, sadistic streak, continued occasionally to produce exquisitely drawn and detailed pictures of spectacular brutality. More often he used a historical theme to illustrate current events. Plate 134, a print intended to be given away with a newspaper to help boost circulation, compared the actor Bando Hikosaburo V, who had recently died, with the twelfth century Taira general Kagekiyo. The analogy depended on the fact that in both cases false rumours circulated after their death that they were actually still alive. Yoshitoshi also drew extensively on Japanese history and legend for his most famous series, the *Hundred Phases of the Moon* (plate 123). Matching his brilliant handling of different styles of drawing to the many various subjects, these hundred prints, each linked by the common motif of the moon, are much admired and avidly collected.

Kiyochika, who was to produce some of the best *senso-e,* war pictures, showing the events of the Sino-Japanese war of 1894, also designed triptychs showing well-known historical tales (plate 133).

Japanese folklore is rich in stories of the supernatural and occult. Pictures of ghostly apparitions and magical transformations were quite popular subjects for the prints, especially in the nineteenth century. These are often found to relate to *kabuki* plays since it was traditional to put on 'spine-chilling' ghost plays during the hot summer months. Such ghosts have long, lank hair, blue or green tinged, pallid faces and no legs. Magical flames are usually shown flickering in the air and whenever such occult fire appears it is certain that supernatural forces are at work (plate 138).

Hokusai, as usual, produced some superb examples (plate 140), while Toyokuni and his pupils, particularly Kunisada and Kuniyoshi, excelled at these evocations of the weird and macabre. No one who is interested in representations of the world of the occult can fail to be fascinated by these prints.

The discovery of the rich fabric of Japanese history and legend is one of the delights of studying the prints. Any effort involved in unravelling the story that is the subject of a print is amply repaid by the new life that is infused into it.

138. (*Opposite above left*) Toyokuni III (Kunisada), *The actor Bando Hikosaburo V as the ghost of O-Iwa*, 1861. *Oban* colour print. Private Collection.
The vengeful ghost of the disfigured, tragic heroine of *Yotsuya Kaidan* (The Ghost of Yotsuya).

139. (*Opposite above right*) Toyokuni III (Kunisada), *The ghost of Yasukata* from *Parodies of the 36 Poets – Nakatsukasa*. 1852. *Oban* colour print. Private Collection.
Without the supernatural flames on the left it might not be immediately apparent that this subtle evocation of depression and melancholy is an actor in the role of a ghost.

140. (*Opposite below left*) Hokusai, *Ghost of Kohada Koheiji* from *One Hundred Tales*, c.1830. *Chuban* colour print. Tokyo National Museum.
A jealous ghost returning to the bed of his former wife and peering over the mosquito net. Only five of the set are known, each a masterpiece of eerie horror. Some unnervingly good facsimiles were printed in 1894.

141. (*Opposite below right*) Kuniyoshi, *The actor Nakamura Utaemon IV as the ghost of Otaka Shuzen*, c.1847. *Oban* colour print. Private Collection.

142. (*Overleaf left*) Kunisada, *The warrior-monk Yokogawa Kakuhan*, c.1830. *Oban* colour print. Private Collection.
During the civil wars of the twelfth century, Yokogawa Kakuhan lead a band of fighting monks against the small group accompanying Yoshitsune who was attempting to flee the jealous emnity of his brother Yoritomo (page 112). Kakuhan was eventually slain and his followers put to flight by a rearguard action by Tadanobu, who had donned Yoshitsune's armour as a ruse to draw off the attack.

143. (*Overleaf right*) Kuniyoshi, *Tammeijiro Genshogo slaying Orin* from *One Hundred and Eight Views of the Popular Suikoden*, c.1827. *Oban* colour print. Private Collection.

横川覺範

9
Surimono, Fan Prints and Special Prints

Surimono

A fine *surimono* is an exquisitely beautiful print intended as a gift from one connoisseur to another. To appreciate its finest qualities it must be held in the hand to feel the soft texture of the thick, velvety *hosho* paper and turned in the light to catch the gleams of gold and silver and see the effects of the blind-printed gauffrage or the sheen of mica. Such a print would be the culmination of the experience of the skilled craftsmen who had striven to produce the finest 'printed thing' (the literal translation of *surimono*) of which their techniques were capable. Originally evolving from the calendar prints, they were privately printed in small editions for the cultured amateurs of the poetry clubs. They were used as greetings cards by individuals or groups on all manner of congratulatory occasions and festivals, especially at the New Year. During the latter part of the eighteenth century many of the famous artists are known to have designed them. Time has swept most of these away and only a few examples remain. From about 1790 Shumman began to specialize in the design of high quality *surimono* to carry poems composed by himself and his friends (plate 148). By the turn of the century Hokusai, using the signatures 'Shunro', 'Sori' and finally 'Hokusai', had joined him in producing the first of a flood of splendid examples which make the next thirty years a fruitful source for the collector. Increasingly artists began to design *surimono* for sale to the general public, both singly and in sets. An almost square shape, *shikishiban,* became the ordinary format, although many other sizes and shapes, both larger and smaller, were produced.

Hokusai continued to pour out a wealth of *surimono* during the first thirty years of the nineteenth century (plate 149). In addition to his Hokusai signature he also signed himself 'Iitsu', 'Tatsuma', 'Taito' and 'One who is crazy about painting'. He was closely followed by his pupils Yanagawa Shigenobu, Shinsai, Hokkei (plate 163) and by Hokkei's pupil Gakutei.

Hiroshige designed only a few *surimono* and none of them are especially distinguished. Kunisada attained a higher standard, especially when he was commissioned to design prints to commemorate a special event in the *kabuki* world, for example a change of name by an actor. Kuniyoshi used a wider range of subjects but his *surimono,* some of which are outstanding, are unfortunately quite rare (plate 158).

144. Harunobu, *Young woman in a sudden shower*, 1765. *Chuban* colour print. Chicago, Art Institute of Chicago. The characters for the long months of 1765 appear on the *kimono* on the washing line. The year is further pin-pointed by characters concealed in the pattern on the girl's *obi*. The signature and seal at the left are those of Hakusei (the amateur who commissioned and conceived the print). At bottom right appear the names of the printer, engraver and artist (Harunobu).

146. (*Above*) Hokusai, *Autumn maple leaves on Tsutaya River* from *One Hundred Poems explained by the Nurse*, c.1839. *Oban* colour print. London, British Museum.
The poem is by Ariwara no Narihira (d.880) 'Waters of Tatsuta, never even in the golden age of old did the gods in their might behold you fairer, laced with the crimson of leaves' (Binyon).

147. (*Left*) Kuniyoshi, *Yoko and the tiger* from *Twenty-four Paragons of Filial Piety*, c.1840. *Oban* colour print. Private Collection.
Yoko was in the forest with his father who fell and injured his leg. A huge tiger appeared and Yoko drew the beast off and was devoured, allowing his father to escape.

145. (*Left*) Kunisada, *Hangaku defending the gate*, mid–1830s. *Oban* colour print. Private Collection.
A warrior heroine who helped defend the stockade when her father's forces were beseiged by Moritsuna in 1201.

Some of the Edo artists are recorded as having some of their designs for *surimono* engraved and printed by the master craftsmen of Osaka. The artists of Osaka who normally had such high standards of printing available produced some fine examples, some of which are in much larger format (plate 152).

As Hillier has shown in 'The Uninhibited Brush' the artists of the academic Shijo, Nanga and allied schools, although mainly working in albums and illustrated books, also ventured into this field. In yet another style, as the nineteenth century advanced, Gengyo and, especially Zeshin were outstanding.

The attraction of *surimono* comes partly from the brilliance of their immaculate printing, partly from the obvious care lavished by the artist on the composition of the design and partly by the aptness of the subject and the poems, where these can be deciphered. Subjects for these prints are very varied: in addition to all the usual girls, actors, landscapes, *kacho-ga* and *shunga* there are also tableaux of still-life. These are often symbolic of good luck, happiness and longevity and may be combined with other symbols suggesting the date or time of year, or may be emblematic of some special occasion or festival. The Japanese delighted in a wayward subtleness on such occasions. It can be appreciated that when the intention was deliberately rendered obscure it is naturally sometimes difficult to perceive more than a fraction of the original message without an intimate knowledge of the language (puns and rebuses occur) and customs of the time.

Collectors of *surimono* have to exercise caution as many of the best were copied. In some cases the harder paper, dull pigments and relatively poor printing make such copies easy to detect. Others, however, have been very skilfully made and could easily deceive all but the most expert unless an undoubted original is available for comparison.

Fan Prints

Fans were a common accoutrement in Japan. 'Every class of person, noble or humble, uses a fan throughout the kingdom', wrote João Rodrigues in 1620, '... perhaps nothing strikes the newly arrived European more than this fan, which he sees in the hand or girdle of every human being.' confirmed the authors of *Manner and Customs of the Japanese* in 1841. Two types of fan were in use: the folding *ogi* pasted onto hinged slats of wood (plate 76) and the rounded *uchiwa*, mounted on a rigid wooden frame (plate 89).

Many of these ephemera were printed and the artists and publishers found in them a further profitable outlet for their work. Comparatively few have survived and those printed prior to the mid-nineteenth century are distinctly rare. Many of the print artists turned their hands to fan design, although none seem to have made these a speciality. The subjects of the designs are not usually different from those current in other formats, actors and courtesans predominating in the eighteenth

century and *bijin-ga, kacho-ga* and landscape in the nineteenth. Considerable ingenuity is sometimes shown by the artists adapting their designs to the contours of the fan shape. While many such prints were made to decorate fans many others are found with a fan-shaped design solely as an artistic device or, occasionally for cutting out and use as decorative panels. A set of prints by Shigenaga and Kiyomasu II illustrating the *Tale of Genji* were published in the mid-1730s. They have the instructions 'Fine designs for a needle-box or sliding door or for pasting on screens' printed on the surround. Similar prints are known by Okumura Masanobu and Toshinobu. The print by Toyokuni (plate 40) shows the sort of effect aimed for on a screen.

Ogi-shaped fans are hardly ever to be found. A few, large uncut sheets of actors by Shunsho and courtesans by Koryusai (plates 154, 155) have been preserved. These have printed instructions for mounting as fans. The smaller print by Shunko (plate 153) was probably not intended for use. In the nineteenth century a few uncut examples by Hiroshige and Kuniyoshi are known.

Uchiwa fan designs are less rare and specimens from the eighteenth century are known by Harunobu, Shigemasa, Buncho, Shunei, Shunko, Shunen, Shunjo, Toyokuni and Utamaro. Utamaro designed a dozen fans, mostly of courtesans, but only one of these appears to have any merit. Toyokuni's designs, although fewer are known, are higher in quality, especially those of actors (plate 156). The bulk of the surviving fan prints stem from the nineteenth century. Those three prolific artists, Hiroshige, Kuniyoshi and Kunisada, with their pupils, notably Sadahide and Fusatane, have left some very pleasing designs, the format often seeming to have provided a challenge which

148. (*Above left*) Shumman, *White and pink peonies with purple iris* from *A Collection of Plants and Trees for the Kasumi Club*, mid-1790s. *Shikishiban surimono*. London, Victoria and Albert Museum.

149. (*Above*) Hokusai, *Crow, sword and plum blossom* from *Four Clans of Japan*, c.1822. *Chuban surimono*. Tokyo National Museum.
The crow and the sword feature in a legend regarding the famous sword that was preserved as an heirloom by the Taira family.

151. (*Right*) Yoshimori, *Nichiren calming the storm
with an invocation*, 1857. *Oban* colour-printed
triptych. London, Victoria and Albert Museum.
Nichiren (1222–82) was a Buddhist saint whose
life was studded with miracles. Threatened by a
storm concocted by an evil spirit while on the way
to exile in Sado, Nichiren calmed the raging
waters with his invocation: *Namu myoho renge kyo*
(the sutra of the lotus of the Wonderful Law).

150. *(Left)* Sadahide, *A dragon and two tigers*, 1858. *Oban* colour-printed triptych. London, Victoria and Albert Museum.
Among their other attributes, the dragon and the tiger represent the forces of clouds and wind which, combined, make the rain.

152. (*Opposite above left*) Sadahiro, *Chasing fire-flies*, c.1840. Large *surimono* 15½ × 20 in (39 × 53 cm). Private Collection.

153. (*Opposite above right*) Shunko, *The actor Iwai Hanshiro IV*, mid-1780s. Small colour-printed *ogi* fan-print. Manchester, Whitworth Art Gallery.

154. (*Opposite below left*) Shunsho, *The actor Nakamura Nakazo II* from *Fans of the East*, 1778. Colour-printed *ogi* fan-print. Tokyo National Museum.
This print was issued to celebrate the new Nakazo, who took over the title in 1778.

155. (*Opposite below right*) Koryusai, *The courtesan Hanaogi (Flower-fan) of the House of the Fan, with an attendant* from *Fans of the East*, c.1778. Colour-printed *ogi* fan-print. Chicago, Art Institute of Chicago.

enabled them to produce artistically attractive prints. Hiroshige designed some fine landscapes (plate 159) and *kacho-ga* and, in the Victoria & Albert Museum, London, more than one hundred and thirty fan prints by him have been assembled. Kuniyoshi (plate 157) and Kunisada (plate 161) mostly used girls and actors as subjects although Kuniyoshi, as usual the more versatile of the two, also included some humorous pictures of cats and other extravagant and witty designs. Hokusai seems to have produced few fan prints. Apart from a set of eight landscape views, there are probably only two, both outstanding, showing birds. Later in the century Kyosai, Zeshin, Gengyo and others produced some exquisitely printed fan-prints, mostly of birds and flowers. Some of these were printed in an octagonal shape.

Other special prints

Most prints were designed simply to be looked at. Some, however, had special features or had an intrinsic, functional purpose.

Harimase sheets, printed with several small designs, were intended to be cut up and pasted on to screens or similar surfaces as decoration. Others, known as *kumitate-e*, when backed on to stiffer paper and cut out could be assembled to construct models, often of *kabuki* sets.

Some prints, mainly from the eighteenth century, were meant to be viewed through a peephole in a box. Itinerants with such contraptions, which sometimes included magnifying lenses and mirrors, would make a living by allowing country folk to view these pictures for a small sum. Some of these prints were printed with the text in reverse, which would, of course, be corrected by the mirrors.

In the mid-nineteenth century there was a vogue for prints which, when pasted on the sides of a square paper lantern, stood out effectively when the lamp was lit. The designs on these prints usually incorporated a scene where an area of the picture, illuminated by a beam from a lantern, appeared in glowing colour, while the background remained shadowy and grey.

Several varieties of games used printed 'boards'. Most often seen is *sukeroku*, where the players moved counters round squares representing the fifty-three stations of the Tokaido.

A different sort of amusement was offered by some nineteenth century-pictures of battle-scenes where cannon blasts and explosions were rendered more realistic by small areas of scattered gunpowder, which exploded when ignited.

Wood-block printing was used extensively for maps, whether street maps of the cities or general maps of Japan and its provinces or world atlases. The first printed world map was published in Nagasaki in 1645. A later, more accurate world map was designed in 1792 by Shiba Kokan and is notable for being engraved on copperplate. Important early mapmakers include Ishikawa Ryusen, a pupil of Moronobu, who produced decorative maps of Japan and Edo in the 1680s, and Nagakubo

156. Toyokuni, *The actor Segawa Kikunojo III*, 1808. Colour-printed *uchiwa* fan-print. 9 × 10¾ in (22.5 × 27 cm). Private Collection.
The actor is shown off-stage and is accompanied by a poem by Jippensha Ikku.

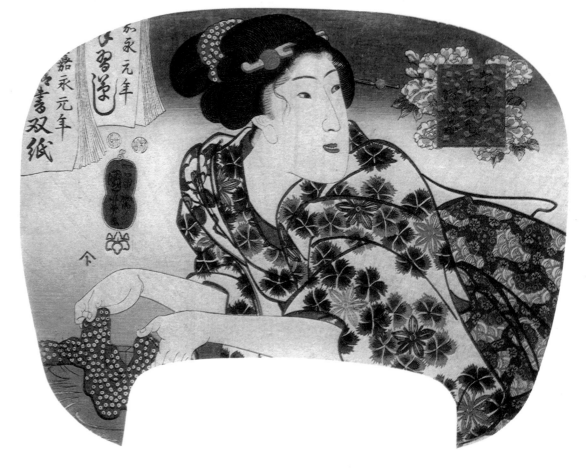

157. Kuniyoshi, *Girl washing a patterned cloth* from *Seven Komachi*, 1848. Colour-printed *uchiwa* fan-print. Private Collection.
The scene is linked with the *soshi arai* episode, where Komachi, accused during a poetry contest of using a poem from an old anthology, washes the paper of the ancient text. Her poem, written into the text by a jealous rival, who had overheard her composing it, washes out since the ink is still fresh.

158. Kuniyoshi, *Girl in a boat by night*,
c.1830. *Shikishiban surimono*. Private
Collection.

159. Hiroshige, *The Naruto rapids in Awa Province* from *Famous places in the Provinces*, mid-1850s. Colour-printed *uchiwa* fan-print. London, Victoria and Albert Museum.
The famous whirlpools and eddies of the tidal rush through the narrows that separate the Inland Sea from the Pacific Ocean occur in several of Hiroshige's most masterly designs of this era.

160. Gakutei, *Court poetess at a writing table*, c.1830. *ogi*-shaped *surimono*. London, Victoria and Albert Museum.

Sekisui, who drew more accurate but less attractive maps in the 1770s. The provinces, especially the more militarily vulnerable coastal areas, were exhaustively surveyed in the early nineteenth century by Ino Tadataka, whose work remained the basis for much of the cartography up to the beginning of the twentieth century.

Kabuki playbills occasionally have illustrations of scenes from the plays listed in the program but usually they show only the *mon* of the principal actors and detailed lists of the actors and their roles (plate

27). They sometimes contain useful information relevant to research into the actor prints.

The song sheet (plate 162), with its delightful scene of the tipsy reveller and a girl accompanying him on the *samisen,* is very evocative of the world of the prints.

Memorial prints, *shini-e,* became popular in the 1820s and most often show actors, who had recently died, dressed in Buddhist robes and holding a rosary. They usually give the actor's professional name, his posthumous name, the date of his death, the temple where he is buried and a laudatory, memorial poem. There must have been considerable demand for such prints at the time. When Iwai Hanshiro VI died in 1836 Kuniyoshi designed at least five different memorial prints for separate publishers. Of even more interest to collectors are the *shini-e* issued when some of the print artists died. Kunisada drew memorial portraits of Toyokuni and Hiroshige. Kunichika, in his turn, drew commemorative portraits of Kunisada. Kuniyoshi featured in two such prints, one, on his own, by Yoshi-iku, the other, when he is shown with his recently deceased pupil Yoshifusa, by Yoshitomi.

Illustrated calendar prints, *e-goyomi,* were produced and given to friends at the New Year. In Japan the twelve months were assigned either twenty-nine days (short months) or thirty days (long months). The arrangement was changed each year and the government issued plainly printed calendars through a few specially licensed publishers. Other publishers, not party to this monopoly, issued, usually for private patrons, prints in which indications of the long and the short months were more or less subtly concealed. The most famous are those produced for the poetry clubs by Harunobu (plate 144). These beautifully designed, luxury calendars are by no means typical of the average *e-goyomi,* which are often rather small prints, whose merit lies in the ingenuity with which the hidden message is concealed.

161. (*Above left*) Kunisada, *The actor Nakamura Shikan II,* 1830. Colour-printed *uchiwa* fan-print. Tokyo National Museum.

162. (*Above*) Anonymous, *Fashionable Song – 'No harmony',* 1850s. *Oban* colour print. Private Collection.
A broadsheet whose prime objective was to publish the words of a new, popular song. The tipsy singer shown bawling out the words, accompanied by a less than reputable serving girl, is brilliantly evocative of the spirit of revelry. The design is in the style of Kuniyoshi.

音陽舘 梅世

くろ
ふいける
れにを
あらく
めぐらふき
角とひ
あとひ
ふらひくり
まき気

163. (Above) Hokkei, *Shoki encouraging a small demon to show off his tricks*, c.1830. *Shikishiban surimono*. London, Victoria and Albert Museum.
The hanging decorations and coloured poetry slips at the top of the print suggest that it was issued for the *Tanabata* festival.

164. (Right) Ashiyuki, *The actor Arashi Rikan II as Mashiba Hisayoshi (Hideyoshi)*, c.1830. *Oban* colour print. Private Collection.
From a tetraptych showing the confrontation between the victorious Hideyoshi and the renegade Akechi Mitsuhide.

10
Other Styles
and Other Places

Besides the popular Edo prints there are four other distinct and separate groups of Japanese graphic art. These are, by comparison, less numerous and less well known but each has its band of enthusiastic devotees. The four groups comprise the 'Osaka prints', the *Nagasaki-e,* the *Yokohama-e* and the prints and albums of the Shijo artists.

The Osaka Prints

Osaka was an important commercial and banking centre and its inhabitants could afford and expected high standards of craftsmanship. One of their principal pleasures was the theatre and the majority of the prints show *kabuki* actors. Despite the considerable contact with developments in Edo, since both actors and artists travelled freely between these centres, the prints produced in Osaka have an individual character which usually renders them unmistakable.

Wood-block printed books had been published in Osaka since the seventeenth century but the prints date almost exclusively from the first half of the nineteenth. Typically they are finely engraved and printed, with pure, opaque pigments on high-quality paper. Editions were small and often for private rather than public circulation and many of the artists were either amateurs or, at most, part-time designers. Certainly by comparison with the professional artists of Edo there were few Osaka artists with any considerable output, even taking into account their penchant for frequent changes of name.

The first prints of note were designed by Ryakosai, Shokosai and Masafusa in the last years of the eighteenth century and the first decade of the nineteenth. These are mostly in *hosoban* format and are rare. It was their pupils and the next generation of artists whose prints really established the Osaka school. An important further stimulus was a series of visits to Osaka by Hokusai, Kunisada and Yanagawa Shigenobu between 1817 and 1822.

The first artist of importance was Shunkosai Hokushu (active 1810–32), whose changes of name are a good example of this habit, which makes the evolution of the school so difficult to follow. He had been a pupil of Shokosai and, when the latter ceased designing prints, in 1809, became Shokosai II for a year or so. From 1812 to 1818 he signed himself Shunko until, after working with Hokusai in 1817, he changed his name to Hokushu. He produced many powerful actor

165. Hokushu, *Actor Nakamura Utaemon III as Ishikawa Goemon,* 1826. *Oban* colour print. Philadelphia, Philadelphia Museum of Art.
Goemon, the villainous, illegitimate son of Akechi Mitsuhide (see plate 54) disguised himself in courtier's robes in an attempt on the life of Hideyoshi, his father's slayer (see plate 164). Foiled, he escapes by magical powers.

異邦蒸氣船出帆之圖
スチームトリ

146

prints that were noted for expressing the heights of theatrical tension that Osaka audiences particularly appreciated in *kabuki* (plate 165). Nearly all the actor portraits have the features contorted in a typical *mie* with squinting eyes but, characteristic of the Osaka prints, the eyes are prominently bulging in a way rarely seen in the prints of Edo.

Nagahide (active 1799–1848), another pupil of Shokosai, produced cheaply printed, stencil-coloured *hosoban* and fan prints. These were ephemeral and are now rare.

Ashikuni (1775–1818), who was a painter, book illustrator and bookseller, produced only about a dozen prints, mainly during his last four years. His influence was considerable however, and he had eleven pupils, each adopting a signature beginning 'Ashi . . .'. Most of these produced only a handful of prints but one of them, Ashiyuki (active 1814–33), was outstanding. He not only produced about two hundred prints, many more than most Osaka artists, but also introduced many innovations. He used the horizontal as well as the upright format, splashed *gofun* (an opaque, white pigment) on his prints to depict snow and produced a contrast in his prints between the actor, drawn in sharp outline and the background, printed in an impressionistic style without outlines (plate 164). He was one of the pioneers in the use of *surimono* techniques of printing on larger prints in the 1830s.

168. (*Above*) Hirosada, *The actor Nakamura Utaemon IV as Higuchi no Jiro*, 1851. *Chuban* colour-printed diptych with gold and silver metallic embellishment. Courtesy of Robin Kennedy, London. The valiant warrior Higuchi no Jiro climbed a tree as an observation post only to find himself surrounded by his enemies.

166. (*Opposite above*) Nagasaki-e (anon.), *Foreign steamships*, c.1845. *Bai-oban* colour print 12 × 17½ in (31 × 44.3 cm). Private Collection.
The white ensign may reflect the visit to Nagasaki of H.M.S. Samarang, a British naval survey vessel in 1845.

167. (*Opposite below*) Yoshitora, *A port in the United States* from *Views of Savage Countries*, 1866. *Oban* colour-printed triptych. London, Victoria and Albert Museum.

169. (*Above*) Shigeharu, *The actor Sawamura Kunitaro II*, c.1830. *Oban* colour print. Private Collection.

170. (*Opposite above*) Hirosada, *The actors Ichikawa Ebizo V as Nippon Daemon and Okawa Hashizo as Nakasaina*, 1848. *Chuban* colour print. Private Collection.

171. (*Opposite below left*) Shigemasa, *Dutchmen and Elephant* from *Ehon busho ichiran*, 1786. *Sumi-e* book-illustration. Private Collection. The Dutch, on their rare visits to Edo, often brought imported exotica as presents for the *Shogun*.

172. (*Opposite below right*) J. vander Schley, *Map of Nagasaki* from Vol. 14 of *Histoire Générale des Voyages*, 1756. Hand-coloured engraving. Private Collection. The map appears to have been drawn from information supplied by E. Kaemfer, who was in Nagasaki from 1690–93 as surgeon to the Dutch East India Company. The key shows that the letters on the map designate areas of predominantly military significance. The fan-shaped island of Deshima (I) is clearly shown.

Kunihiro (active 1815–43), who had studied under Toyokuni II and Ashikuni, produced good actor prints in the prevailing style. Shigeharu (1803–53), who called himself Kunishige from 1820–6, became a pupil of Yanagawa Shigenobu and took the name Shigeharu in 1826. Contemporary accounts say that he was the only full-time professional designer of actor prints in Osaka. He was certainly one of the leading artists until the middle 1830s and specialized in actors in striking and dramatic poses (plate 169). It is uncertain whether the artist signing himself Kunishige in the late 1840s is the same man since Shigeharu is said to have returned to his native Nagasaki after the civil uprisings in Osaka at the time of the Tempo famine (1832–6).

Yoshikuni (active 1803–c.1840) studied under Ashikuni and was, for a while, a minor follower of Utamaro. He changed the characters with which he wrote his signature several times during his career and this is sometimes helpful in dating his prints. His most successful figure designs, which include a few fine bust portraits of actors, come from the 1820s. His pupil Shibakuni (active 1821–6) also produced some excellent bust portraits and some above-average figure designs. His work seems rare.

Of Hokushu's pupils, Hokucho and Hokuei are of note. Hokucho (active 1822–30) was a competent artist who specialized in polyptychs. Hokuei (active 1824–37) was one of the most important and prolific artists of the 1830s. With Shigeharu and Ashiyuki he perfected the use of the new saturated earth pigments and, with metallic pigments and careful embossing, produced some of the finest *surimono*-type *oban* prints. These elaborate and luxurious prints seem to have been banned in 1838 and did not fully revive until the late 1840s.

Kunisada's visit to Osaka in 1821 seems to have made little immediate impact but he did influence several artists. In 1828 Sadahiro (active 1825–51) travelled to Edo to study with him for a while. Sadahiro designed some landscapes and large *surimono* (plate 152) as well as actor prints. Some controversy surrounds his career but it seems almost certain that he owned the Tenki publishing house from 1835–52 and that from 1847 he reversed the characters of his signature, changing his name to Hirosada. Sadamasu designed landscapes in the 1830s and changed his name to Kunimasu in 1844 and later produced *chuban* actor prints. Sadanobu (1809–79) produced some pleasing landscapes in the style of the later Hiroshige prints of the 1850s.

Since the main subject material of the prints was the actors, when the edicts of 1842 banned them, a blight fell on the output of the publishing houses of Osaka for nearly five years. The penalties attached to these laws were so severe that it must have required considerable courage when Hirosada, under a pseudonym, published an actor print early in 1847. When this was allowed to pass unchallenged Hirosada immediately began to produce the large numbers of prints mainly in the *chuban* format which eventually made him the most prolific of all the

173. Chinnen, *Young woman threading a needle*, c.1830. *Chuban* colour print. Private Collection.
There is a wealth of wry humour in this simple design. The old woman stares accusingly at her glasses while the younger woman smugly prepares to thread the needle.

174. (*Opposite*) Hasui, *Snow at Mukaijima*, 1931. *Oban* colour print. Private Collection.

150

Osaka artists. He utilized all the superb printing refinements traditionally available in Osaka. While the artistic quality of his prints is variable, the best are very good and his combination of fine design and outstanding printing made him the dominant force between 1847 and 1852 (plates 168, 170). Many artists imitated him during the 1850s and 1860s until Osaka print production gradually ceased. Most notable during this last phase were Yoshitaki, Kunikazu, Kunishige and Munehiro.

Nagasaki-e
'O Wad some Pow'r the giftie gie us
To see oursels as others see us!'
(Robert Burns)
Curiosity about the stranger from foreign parts, mixed with other emotions according to circumstances, is common to all peoples and the

阿蘭陀人馬術之圖

阿蘭陀人男女之圖

175. (*Above*) *Nagasaki-e* (anon.), *Dutch horseman*, early nineteenth century. *O-hosoban* colour print. London, British Museum.

176. (*Above right*) *Nagasaki-e* (anon.), *Dutch man and woman*, early nineteenth century. *Chuban* colour print. London, British Museum.

Japanese were no exception. Even a glance at plate 171 can leave no doubt about the intense interest evoked by the two Dutchmen and the strange animal that they have brought with them. All accounts of the early travellers to Japan confirm that this interest extended to every detail of themselves and their possessions.

An almost total, self-imposed seclusion, that effectively prevented intercourse between Japan and the rest of the world, was enforced from the early seventeenth century until the 1850s. The earliest recorded contact between Europeans and the Japanese was in 1543, when three Portuguese landed after being blown off course. They were followed in 1549 by the missionary Francis Xavier and then by traders from all the sea-faring nations. After many years of erratic but generally mutually satisfactory trade, the Japanese rulers became increasingly and justifiably alarmed by reports of their colonizing processes. Elsewhere priests had been followed by traders who would call on military force to protect their interests, with subsequent annexation. Early in the seventeenth

century the Tokugawa clan, newly emerged from the civil wars that had brought them to power, were determined to ensure their own absolute rule. In 1611 the first anti-Christian edicts were promulgated. The persecutions that followed reached their peak in 1625, when torture and executions both of foreign priests and Japanese converts were commonplace. The Dutch and English, whose low-key Protestant faith posed a lesser threat than the proselytizing, Catholic Spanish and Portuguese, intrigued successfully against their rivals. But the English left in 1623 and, when the final exclusion orders were enforced in 1639, there were left only a dozen Dutchmen and some Chinese, who were allowed to live at the distant port of Nagasaki, originally constructed by the Portuguese. The Dutch were confined, not on the sacred soil of Japan, but on the artificially created, three-acre island of Deshima, which the Shogun had ordered to be built in the shape of a fan (plate 172). A narrow, guarded bridge led from the island to the waterfront of Nagasaki. The town was ruled by commissioners under the direct supervision of the Shogun, who thereby controlled all trade and vetted all information that filtered into or out of the port. Very occasionally a Dutch envoy was compelled to make the long journey to Edo and was obliged to crawl into the presence of the Shogun and offer him gifts.

This minute Dutch encampment was to be Japan's only link with the Western world for the next two hundred years. For most of this time only two Dutch ships were permitted to enter each year and these principally brought cargoes of exports from Java. Their presence, however, excited great interest and led *inter alia* to both paintings and prints showing both the Dutch and the Chinese; their tall, black, ocean-going vessels; maps and topographical scenes of Nagasaki itself. The Dutch, being more outlandish, were more often figured, the artists noting their

177. Yoshikazu, detail from *The Interior of an American Ship*, 1861. From an *oban* colour-printed triptych. Private Collection.

154

'high noses, blue eyes, red hair, white skins and tall bodies' together with their seemingly extraordinary clothes.

The presence of artists in Nagasaki was not accidental since the government employed copyists to reproduce line for line all pictures and paintings that were imported, which were predominantly Chinese works. It is supposed that the Nagasaki prints were designed by such men as a sideline. The prints were usually unsigned and of those few that do carry a signature (mostly from the nineteenth century), little is known of the artists. These prints were published and sold in Nagasaki itself – presumably as souvenirs. The printing techniques were similar to those used in Edo, although the sizes of paper used were often larger and the pigments were slightly different; a pale brown and a vivid blue are especially typical. They all seem to be decidedly rare.

Yokohama-e

If the *Nagasaki-e* showed the handful of Dutch and Chinese traders, allowed a tiny foothold many hundreds of miles from Edo, the

179. Shoun (1870–1965), *Winter scene* from *The Four Seasons*, c.1900. *Oban* colour print. Private Collection.
In late Meiji times, the technical achievements of handling the multiple colour blocks perfectly graded and registered reached an apogee. This print also shows the effective use of blind printing to add texture and pattern to the garments. The appearance of fine, falling snow is produced by spray-on opaque white pigment applied after the rest was printed.

178. (*Opposite*) Shinsui, *Girl washing linen*, 1917. *Oban* colour print. London, British Museum.

155

180. Kunitoshi, *The new railway station* from *Famous Views of Edo*, early 1870s. *Oban* colour print. Private Collection. The first railway in Japan, from Yokohama to Edo, was opened in 1872.

Yokohama-e commemorate the flood of merchants and officials from all the major trading nations that flocked to the newly opened treaty ports in the 1860s. The threat of the guns of Commodore Perry's American warships had led to a limited trading treaty in 1854. The Japanese government was in disarray, weakened and divided by conflicting factions. It took a further five years of diplomacy and threats before definitive treaties with the United States, Great Britain, Holland, Russia and France, the 'five nations', allowed for extra-territorial jurisdiction, fixed customs tariffs, permanent diplomatic envoys in Edo and the opening of a port at Yokohama, less than twenty miles from the capital.

The intense interest aroused by these events was due partly to the natural curiosity of the inhabitants of Edo, who had rarely seen Europeans or their wares and partly to the political ructions that the arrival of the foreigners stirred. Factions working to topple the Shogun's government incited anti-foreign feeling. In 1859 and 1860 murderous assaults on foreign traders in Yokohama coincided with conspiracies against the government and political assassinations. None of these latter events show up in the *Yokohama-e,* although they are occasionally referred to obliquely in some of the contemporary *musha-e* triptychs.

The *Yokohama-e* show pictures of the new port, the paddle-steamers in the harbour, the traders and their warehouses and impressions of the foreign places from where they had come.

The artists who drew them came from Edo and were mostly pupils of Kuniyoshi, Kunisada and Hiroshige. Most notable were Sadahide, Yoshitora, Yoshikazu and Hiroshige II, although at least a score of other artists contributed to the genre. Sadahide (1807–73) was one of the first to draw the Americans and their warships and he may have been commissioned by the government to do this even before Yokohama was opened in 1859. He was a fine draughtsman and often managed to bring a flair for compositional design to his pictures, when many of his contemporaries relied solely on pictorial reporting. Yoshitora (active 1850–80) produced many triptychs of the port and the trading ships and single-sheet prints showing slightly wooden representations of the merchants and officers of the various nations. Later, doubtless based on imported Western engravings, he designed some interesting triptychs of scenes from foreign lands. Plate 167 shows an American port and other similar views show London, Paris and Nankin. Yoshikazu (active 1850–70), one of the most prolific Yokohama artists, covered the whole field and was often most successful showing groups of foreigners, whether relaxing in the tea-houses of Yokohama or parading in the streets or, as in plate 177, aboard their vessels. Hiroshige II has mentioned in the chapter on landscape and his training by Hiroshige undoubtedly stood him in good stead when it came to depicting the brick built hotels and legations and the other marvels that the.Westerners introduced to Japan.

The vast majority of *Yokohama-e* worthy of the name come from the period 1860–70, especially the first two or three years of the decade. Thereafter it required some particularly newsworthy event, such as the visit of the French circus in 1871 or the opening of the Yokohama-Edo steam railway a year later, to send the artists scurrying off, sketch-book in hand, like news reporters. All the prints were published in Edo by the same craftsmen, using the same techniques, as usually produced the other Edo broadsheets. Artistically these prints are rarely of great note. Their merit is mainly derived from their status as fascinating historical curios.

Prints by the Classical Schools of Painting

The albums of the artists of the Nanga schools, derived from the ideals of 'Southern' Chinese painting and their native offshoots, especially the Shijo and Maruyama schools, were produced for a small, discerning circle of literati. Their impressionistic styles attempted to capture the inner spirit of the subjects and appealed to the more wealthy, cultured amateurs of Kyoto and Osaka.

Many of the albums were intended as painting manuals for such men and others were anthologies contributed by groups of amateurs and doubtless intended for private circulation among their friends. The numbers of artists whose work can be found published in this way runs into thousands, many of whom are known by only one or two designs. About a hundred and fifty were more prolific and seem to have been at least semi-professional painters or teachers. These artists are important to studies of eighteenth and nineteenth century Japanese painting and book illustration but, although some, mainly in the nineteenth century, used the wood-block publishers to print *surimono,* none published prints for the commercial markets and any detailed survey of their work is beyond the scope of this book.

The pictures in the albums, often only swift sketches, were, however, designed to be printed and are seldom an attempt to reproduce finished paintings. They were mostly printed without an outline keyblock and,

181. (*Above left*) Goshun (1752–1811) and Yacho (1782–1828), *Festival dancers,* c.1810. Large album print. London, Victoria and Albert Museum.
The girls on the left are by Goshun (signed Gekkei), the founder of the Shijo style, the trio on the right by Yacho, one of Goshun's pupils.

182. (*Above*) Chinnen (1792–1851), *The gardener,* mid-1830s. Colour print 13¾ × 12¼ in (32.4 × 31.1 cm). Private Collection.
The quiet absorption of the man, gently separating his plants for potting, contrasts with the frenetic dance of the dragon-flies above his head.

183. Shoson (Koson), *Heron in the snow*, mid–1930s. *O-tanzaku* colour print. Private Collection.

by careful engraving and printing, endeavours were made to reproduce the effect of a charged brush drawn across the paper.

The subjects were predominantly nature studies (plate 132) or Chinese-inspired landscapes. Figure studies were mostly designed to convey events or activities rather than to act as portraits of personalities (plates 173, 181, 182). There was no attempt to imitate the Edo pictures of actors or courtesans and erotic prints are scarcely ever found. This is hardly surprising considering the Confucian-based philosophy to which the clientele of these albums aspired. The subject was, however, always secondary to the brushwork. It was the style and feeling of the result that mattered, leaving much to the imagination and insight of the viewer.

184. Zeshin, *Crows in flight*, 1887. *Shikishiban* colour print. Private Collection.

159

11
Modern Prints

The modern era in Japan can conveniently be regarded as commencing with the reinstatement of the Emperor Meiji in 1868. Contact with the West was now fully established and the internal political upheavals of the 1860s had largely settled. The Japanese set about studying and adapting the foreign achievements in industry, science and the arts to their own use. The 1870s were not a good time for Japanese prints. The popular prints, after a flurry of activity reporting the arrival of the foreigners, seemed to lose their direction and their market appeal. The Shijo artists seemed to have exhausted their ideas and the commonly used aniline dyes were the antithesis of what was wanted to convey their pictures. What kept the art going was the presence of a few men of talent and stubborn individuality. Yoshitoshi continued to produce popular broadsheets, increasing his market by designing prints which were issued as 'colour supplements' for popular newspapers (plate 123). He was a superb draughtsman and possessed of a vivid and often macabre imagination and his prints continued to sell out on publication until, towards the end of his life, he became insane. Zeshin and Koyosai, both eclectic and, in their different ways, continuing the vital spark of Japanese art, contributed some fine prints. Kiyochika and his followers, all active in the 1880s, incorporated some of the new perspectives derived from Western realism and photography.

The Sino-Japanese war of 1894–5 and, a decade later, the Russo-Japanese war temporarily gave a boost to the popular prints and *senso-e,* war pictures, mostly in the form of triptychs, had a vogue before they were totally eclipsed by the photographs of the war correspondents.

By the turn of the century Chikanobu, Gekko, Kogyo, Toshikata and other pupils of Yoshitoshi seem to have split their endeavours into two, producing, on the one hand, pictures of current interest for the newspapers and, on the other, the occasional, more finished work, for publishers who were now trading for a smaller clientele of art-lovers. During the early decades of this century it was the publishers of these latter prints who kept the skills of the wood-block craftsmen alive – often by working on beautifully finished reprints of the earlier masters. These were now in demand following renewed interest in Japanese prints in Europe and America. The original prints which emanated from these publishers, while showing marked differences in treatment from their forerunners, fall into the broad, traditional categories of birds

185. Goyo, *The model Tomi in a blue, floral robe combing her hair*, 1920. *Oban* colour print. London, British Museum.

162

and flowers, beauties and landscapes.

The most commonly encountered artist of birds and flowers of this era is Shoson (1877–1945). His predecessors of a generation earlier, Bairei, Keinen and Taki Katei (plate 111) were still firmly in the mainstream of Japanese art but Shoson, with the encouragement of the American Ernest Fenollosa, then professor of art at Tokyo Imperial University, used a realistic style, basing his designs closely on sketches from life. These were then engraved using the unsurpassed wood-block techniques. In about 1911 he discarded his earlier art name Koson and concentrated on painting until 1926 when, signing himself Shoson, he recommenced his output of prints with the publisher Watanabe. Some of his work borders on the trite but his best designs are superb (plate 183).

It was the publisher Watanabe who encouraged most of those artists who created what became known as the 'new prints'. The most famous are those who specialized in pictures of beauties. Throughout the 1920s and 1930s, Shinsui (1898–1977) (plates 178, 186), Kotondo (b. 1900) and Kiyoshi (1898–1948) designed prints of girls in a delicate neo-*ukiyo-e* style, often with a mildly erotic tinge. Goyu (1880–1921), working mostly along the same lines, felt dissatisfied with the commercial publishing and set up his own studio and personally supervised the engraving and printing of his prints, which were usually issued in fairly small editions. When he died only fourteen of his designs had been published and the prints published in his lifetime are, therefore, relatively rare. After his death some of his unfinished designs were completed and posthumously published by his family.

The most successful and prolific landscape artists were Hasui (1883–1957) and Hiroshi Yoshida (1896–1950). Hasui began to produce prints in 1918 and had had more than sixty designs published by 1923, when a great earthquake and fire devastated Tokyo and destroyed most of his stock of prints and the wood-blocks. These early prints are therefore distinctly rare. He went on to travel extensively throughout Japan, sketching all the while and has left several hundred prints illustrating every aspect of season and climate in Japan (plate 174). Yoshida also travelled widely and his prints are not confined to views of Japan as he also produced sets of scenes of China, India, the U.S.A. and Switzerland. He too took great pains to supervise the engraving and printing, sometimes cutting the blocks himself.

The world of the theatre declined as a source of material for prints. In about 1900 Kogyo (1869–1927) produced a finely printed set showing the *noh* drama. In the early 1920s Toyonari (1885–1942) started producing 'large head' *kabuki* portraits, often with mica backgrounds. Between 1925 and 1930 Natori Shunsen (1886–1960) followed with about fifty striking large actor portraits (plate 187). Both these artists are said to have been much influenced by studying the prints of Sharaku (plate 39).

186. (*Opposite above left*) Shinsui, *Girl with fan*, 1924. *Oban* colour print. London, British Museum.

187. (*Opposite above right*) Natori Shunsen, *The actor Ichikawa Ennosuke II*, 1926. *Oban* colour print. London, British Museum.
The stocky but vigorous character of Ennosuke comes over clearly. He was famous for his acrobatic dancing and extraordinary command of technical tricks in his acting.

188. (*Opposite below left*) Koitsu (b.1870), *Lake Kawaguchi at the foot of Mount Fuji*, 1938. *Oban* colour print. Private Collection.

189. (*Opposite below right*) Elizabeth Keith, *Oriental Market*, c.1920. *Oban* colour print. Private Collection.

190. (*Above*) Urushibara, *Tulips in a vase*, 1920s. 16½ × 13 in (42 × 33 cm) colour print. Private Collection.

191. (*Opposite*) Sekino, *Night in Montmartre*, 1959. Colour print. Dr & Mrs James B. Austin Collection.

A number of European artists came to Japan and used the traditional craftsmanship to produce prints of their own. Notable among these are Elizabeth Keith, who had prints made of sketches of her tour of Korea about 1920 (plate 189), and the French artist Paul Jacoulet who produced pictures of women and scenes of the Far East and the South Pacific. The Japanese artist Urushibara (1888–1953), who spent nearly thirty years in London and Paris, used the traditional methods to publish many delightful European subjects and still-life pictures (plate 190).

From about 1914 some Japanese artists, who had been studying contemporary European artistic methods, began to both carve and print their own prints. As a group they took the view that the creation of the prints was an important part of an artist's work and that something would be lost if an outsider were allowed to print them. Calling their prints *sosaku hanga*, 'creative prints', they formed an association and, after years of struggle against ridicule, they were finally accepted in Japan and began to receive international acclaim. As one might expect, many of these continue to show a distinct Japanese flavour but many others show no indication of their origin. Often the prints are non-representational. In common with similar contemporary art in other lands, controversy continues about whether this type of print, sometimes executed with draughtsmanship of slipshod simplicity, will be judged valuable or valueless in the future. For the present, opinion must rest with the individual.

From its inception, however, the creative art movement has included many artists of undoubted merit. Its most influential founder was Koshiro Onchi (1891–1955) and he and his pupil Junichiro Sekino (b.1914) (plate 191) are both examples of artists who have achieved international fame. There has been a great burgeoning of activity since the 1950s and there are at this moment several hundred Japanese artists working through the medium of the print.

When considering twentieth century art, whether in Japan or elsewhere, the large number of artists and their works of art makes discrimination difficult and renders generalization dangerous. Nevertheless it is quite clear that this century has seen the production of many superb prints by Japanese artists, many of which have a more immediate appeal to the Western eye than the often more arcane prints of the seventeenth and eighteenth centuries. The Japanese have always shown a natural sensitivity to the beauty of colour, form and line, which are the basis of any print. One can only counsel the reader to find and enjoy the best prints of to-day, the ones that give him pleasure, and look forward to those of the future, for the past has no monopoly of talent and we need not doubt that there will be splendid prints to come.

Collecting

There is a special pleasure to be derived from the actual ownership of a work of art. To find, collect and preserve something of beauty and interest, especially when it manifests the supreme achievements of skilled craftsmen, is an experience with many rewards.

Japanese prints are still available in relatively large numbers and are not yet so expensive as to have become the prerogative only of the very rich. Those who are attracted should seize every opportunity to see more prints, as it is only by the careful examination of many prints that powers of discrimination can be developed. It is certainly necessary to distinguish original prints from copies and fakes and to be aware of the significance of variations in states and impressions. Many of the most famous prints were carefully re-engraved and copied from the 1890s onwards but only the most naive would mistake the stiffer, harder paper and modern pigments for an original. Forgeries do exist, designed deliberately to deceive and these vary from pirated copies produced at the same time as the original, to quite modern attempts at fraud. These have been known to fool even the most expert and line by line comparison of a suspected print with an acknowledged genuine example may be needed to dispel final doubt. Such painstaking faking usually only applies, of course, to those famous and sought-after masterpieces that bring the highest prices. Varying states of prints, especially differences in colouring, may reflect different editions or may simply indicate experiments by the printer (plate 10). Some guidance may be gained from careful scrutiny of the engraved lines, which become increasingly broken and thicker with large or multiple editions, as the wood-block became worn.

The condition of a print will markedly affect its value. A grubby, faded, trimmed, late impression will be worth but a tiny fraction of the value of a pristine, early printing. Prices vary enormously and it is only by experience that it is possible to assess accurately a print's value. Here it is instructive to browse through the stock of specialist dealers and to attend auction sales. Some of the larger auction houses hold regular sales of Japanese prints and the opportunity to inspect the prints closely and then see them sold at a price that represents the united opinion of many experienced dealers and collectors is especially valuable. Those too distant to view and attend such sales can easily obtain catalogues from auctioneers such as Sotheby's of London. It is always difficult to assess a proper bid without prior viewing but often a fellow collector or professional agent can be prevailed upon to view, advise and bid on one's behalf.

Prints, once obtained, need to be protected and preserved. Framing and exposure to the light leads slowly but inexorably to severe fading of the colours. Most owners wish to be able to display their treasures and it is probably best to mount the prints on specially selected, stout cardboard to give rigid protection and allow ease of handling. Poor-grade card can cause chemical damage to the paper. Once mounted the prints can be kept in drawers or on shelves to be shown or studied safely. Amateur restoration work is best avoided. Washing a print usually leads to detectable alteration in the texture of the paper and some of the pigments run. Backing the prints is usually unnecessary and, if required, either to strengthen a creased centre-fold or to repair a tear or wormholes, this is best left to an expert restorer. Attempts to freshen the colour of a partly faded print by recourse to a paint-box are almost invariably disastrous and always readily detectable.

There are few incentives greater than the ownership of a print to lead one to its detailed study. The field is so wide that only a small proportion of prints will be found adequately described in a reference work. Despite an extensive bibliography, the prints are nowhere listed in full and only a few individual artists have anything even approaching a *catalogue raisonné*. A knowledge of written Japanese, while obviously useful, is a counsel of perfection but most collectors soon learn to recognize many of the signatures (see appendix) and some of the more common characters found in title cartouches. With the aid of a Japanese character dictionary and some of the reference books listed in the bibliography, it is surprising how much useful information can be gleaned without any detailed knowledge of the language. If the search for information about his prints leads the collector into the realms of Japanese literature, poetry, history and folklore, there are new pleasures in store for him. Indeed, each collector can choose his own field of interest and explore it to whatever depth he pleases. It remains only to wish him good luck and much pleasure in the quest.

Series
sub-title

Series title

Artist's
signature on
the print
within the
print

Number in
series of
prints

Censor seals

Artist's
signature

Date seal

'Ga'
(Drawn by)

Artist's seal

Printer's seal

192. Kuniyoshi, *Girl and cat* from *Beauties of mountain and
sea – Etchu province*, 1852. *Oban* colour print. Private
Collection. The inset view is of octopus fishing at
Namerikawa in Etchu province. It is by Yoshitori, the art
name of Kuniyoshi's daughter, Otori.

Examples of Signatures

Ashikuni · Ashiyuki · Buncho · Chikanobu · Choki · Eiri (Chokyosai) · Eiri (Rekisentei) · Eisen · Eishi · Eisho · Eisui · Eizan · Enjaku · Enkyo · Fusatane · Gakutei

Gekko · Gokyo · Goyo · Harunobu · Harushige · Hasui · Hidemaro · Hirokage · Hirosada · Hiroshige · Hokkei · Hokucho · Hokuei · Hokuju · Hokusai · Hokushu

Keisai (Eisen) · Kikumaru · Kiyochika · Kiyohiro · Kiyomasu · Kiyomine · Kiyomitsu · Kiyonaga · Kiyonobu · Kiyoshige · Kiyotada · Kogyo · Koitsu · Koryusai · Koson · Kotondo

Kuniaki · Kunichika · Kuniharu · Kunihiro · Kunihisa · Kunikage · Kunikazu · Kunimaru · Kunimasa · Kunimasu · Kuninaga · Kuninao · Kunisada · Kunishige · Kuniteru · Kunitora

Kuniyasu · Kuniyoshi · Kyosai · Mangetsudo · Kitao Masanobu · Okumura Masanobu · Masayoshi · Munehiro · Nagahide · Sadafusa · Sadahide · Sadahiro · Sadakage · Sadamasu · Sadanobu · Sadatora

Sharaku · Shibakuni · Shigeharu · Shigemasa · Shigenaga · Nishimura Shigenobu · Shigenobu (Hiroshige II) · Yanagawa Shigenobu · Shiko · Shinsai · Shinsui · Shoson · Shoun · Shucho · Shumman · Shuncho

Shundo · Shunei · Shunjo · Shunko · Kashosai Shunsen · Katsukawa Shunsen · Natori Shunsen · Shunsho · Shuntei · Shunzan · Sugakudo · Toshihide · Toshikata · Toshinobu · Toyoharu · Toyohiro

(Early) Toyokuni · Toyokuni II · Toyokuni III · Toyonari · Toyonobu · Toyoshige · Tsukimaro · Urushibara · Early Utamaro (Ga) · Utamaro (Fude) · Yoshichika · Yoshida · Yoshiiku · Yoshikazu · Yoshikuni

Yoshimaru · Yoshimitsu · Yoshimori · Yoshinobu · Yoshitaki · Yoshitora · Yoshitoshi · Zeshin

169

Date and Censor Seals

Censor seals and date seals often help to date the prints. The *kiwame* seal (1, 2) was introduced in the ninth month of 1790 and occurs on most prints until 1842. In 1805 additional seals showing the number of the month of publication appear and continue until the fourth month of 1806 (3–8). From the fifth month of 1806 until 1811 the year is designated by its zodiacal symbol with a numeral for the month (9–14, numerals omitted to avoid confusion). Between 1811–14 various *gyoji* seals appear (not illustrated, see example plate 40). From the seventh month of 1842 to the end of 1846 single *nanushi* censor seals appear (15–26) and from early 1847–1852 these occur in pairs (27–35). From the second month of 1852 to the eleventh month of 1853 an added date seal gives the year and month (36–43). From the last month of 1853 to the end of 1857 the *aratame* seal replaces the nanushi seals (44–47). In 1858 the date seal appears alone (48). From 1859–71 a single seal combining *aratame*, the zodiacal year symbol and a number denoting the month (mostly omitted from the table) occurs (49–62). Between 1872 and 1875 a simple year-month date seal is found (63–65). From 1876 formal censorship ceased but dates are often given by reference to the years of the Emperor's reign (66–68).

It should be noted that in the date seals the characters used for both the zodiac and the numbers of the months are often given in archaic or abbreviated forms and will often show some variation from the illustration given according to their arrangement in the seal. Seals on fan-prints are sometimes different in shape and date seals may be found at other dates (plate 161). To place these within the correct twelve year zodiacal cycle requires help from internal evidence. The Japanese calendar of this era tends to accord with the Gregorian to within a month or two. Occasionally an extra month was interpolated in a year to correct the calendar.

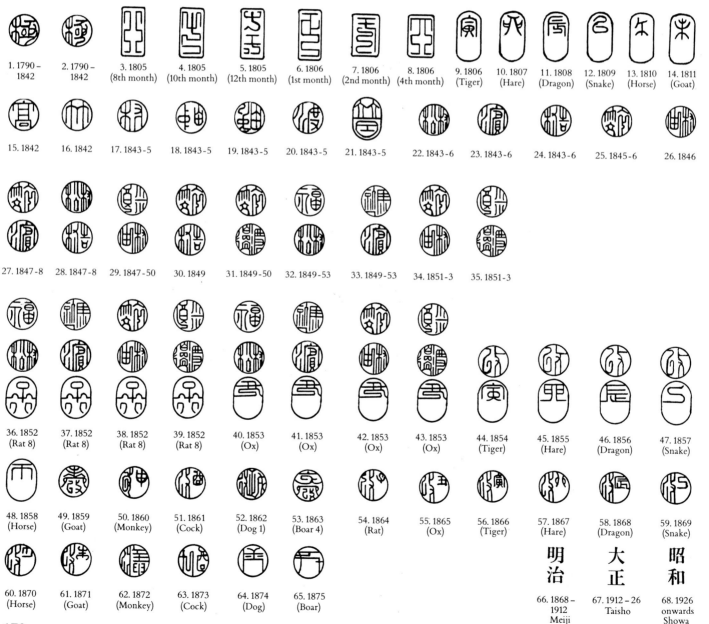

1. 1790–1842 2. 1790–1842 3. 1805 (8th month) 4. 1805 (10th month) 5. 1805 (12th month) 6. 1806 (1st month) 7. 1806 (2nd month) 8. 1806 (4th month) 9. 1806 (Tiger) 10. 1807 (Hare) 11. 1808 (Dragon) 12. 1809 (Snake) 13. 1810 (Horse) 14. 1811 (Goat)

15. 1842 16. 1842 17. 1843-5 18. 1843-5 19. 1843-5 20. 1843-5 21. 1843-5 22. 1843-6 23. 1843-6 24. 1843-6 25. 1845-6 26. 1846

27. 1847-8 28. 1847-8 29. 1847-50 30. 1849 31. 1849-50 32. 1849-53 33. 1849-53 34. 1851-3 35. 1851-3

36. 1852 (Rat 8) 37. 1852 (Rat 8) 38. 1852 (Rat 8) 39. 1852 (Rat 8) 40. 1853 (Ox) 41. 1853 (Ox) 42. 1853 (Ox) 43. 1853 (Ox) 44. 1854 (Tiger) 45. 1855 (Hare) 46. 1856 (Dragon) 47. 1857 (Snake)

48. 1858 (Horse) 49. 1859 (Goat) 50. 1860 (Monkey) 51. 1861 (Cock) 52. 1862 (Dog 1) 53. 1863 (Boar 4) 54. 1864 (Rat) 55. 1865 (Ox) 56. 1866 (Tiger) 57. 1867 (Hare) 58. 1868 (Dragon) 59. 1869 (Snake)

60. 1870 (Horse) 61. 1871 (Goat) 62. 1872 (Monkey) 63. 1873 (Cock) 64. 1874 (Dog) 65. 1875 (Boar) 66. 1868–1912 Meiji 67. 1912–26 Taisho 68. 1926 onwards Showa

170

Glossary

Aiban: print size, about 13½ × 8¾ in (34 × 22 cm).

Aizuri-e: prints coloured predominantly or entirely in shades of blue. Mostly seen in prints of the late 1820s to early 1840s.

Bai-oban: print size, about 18 × 13½ in (46 × 34 cm).

Beni-e: prints hand-coloured in the early to mid-eighteenth century, a pale pink (*beni*) often predominating.

Beni-girai: pink-avoiding prints. Colour prints using a restricted palette or pale pastel shades. Mostly found in prints published about 1790.

Benizuri-e: pink-printed pictures. Produced from mid-1740s to mid-1760s, usually with two-colour blocks in pink and green.

Bijin-ga: pictures of beautiful women.

Chuban: print size, about 10¼ × 7½ in (26 × 19 cm).

Chu-tanzaku: print size, about 15 × 5 in (38 × 13 cm).

Ehon: a picture book.

Ga: 'drawn by', a suffix to signatures.

Go: pseudonym used by an artist.

Hashira-e: print size, about 27½–29½ × 4¾–6 in (70–75 × 12–15 cm). A pillar-print.

Hitsu: 'drawn by', a suffix to signatures.

Hosoban: print size, about 13 × 5¾ in (33 × 14.5 cm).

Kacho-ga: pictures of flowers and birds.

Kakemono-e: print size, about 29½ × 10 in (75 × 25 cm).

Koban: print size, about 9 × 6¾ in (23 × 17 cm).

Kyoka: a short humerous verse.

Mitate: a parody.

Mon: an identifying badge or crest.

Monogatari: tale or story.

Musha-e: pictures of warriors.

Naga-ban: print size, about 19¾ × 9 in (50 × 23 cm).

Oban: print size, about 15 × 10 in (38 × 25 cm). The standard format.

Okubi-e: bust portrait.

O-tanzaku: print size, about 15 × 6¾ in (38 × 17 cm).

Shikishiban: print size, about 8¼ × 7 in (21 × 18 cm). Mostly used for *surimono*.

Shunga: erotic pictures.

Sumi-e: a picture in black and white.

Surimono: a limited edition de luxe print for a special occasion.

Tan-e: prints hand-coloured with red lead (*tan*) and other pigments. Popular from about 1670–1720.

Tanzaku: shape of paper popular for poems. See *chu-tanzaku* and *o-tanzaku*.

Uki-e: pictures incorporating European perspective.

Ukiyo-e: pictures of the 'floating world'. Generic term used to describe pictures of the gay plebeian world of Edo.

Urushi-e: *beni-e* with the addition of glue to the pigments to give a lustrous finish, often with sprinkled metallic dust or mica. A 'lacquer' print.

Yoko-e: horizontal format.

Bibliography

The following list consists of books, mainly with English text, which have mostly been published or reprinted within the last ten years.

General:

Binyon, L. and Sexton, J.J. O'Brien: *Japanese Colour Prints*, London, 1923.

Chibbett, D.G.: *The History of Japanese Printing and Book-Illustration*, Tokyo and Palo Alto, Cal., 1977.

Edmunds, W.H.: *Pointers and Clues to the Subjects of Chinese and Japanese Art*, London, 1935.

Hillier, J.: *The Japanese Print: A New Approach*, London, 1960.

Hillier, J.: *Japanese Prints and Drawings from the Vever Collection*, 3 Vols., London, 1976.

Hillier, J. and Smith, L.: *Japanese Prints in Hiding – The Unexplored Art of Illustrated Albums and Books*, London, 1980.

Illing, R.: *Japanese Prints from 1700 to 1900*, London, 1976.

Illing, R.: *Later Japanese Prints*, London, 1978.

Joly, H.L.: *Legend in Japanese Art*, London and New York, 1908.

Koop, A. and Inada, H.: *Japanese Names and How to Read Them*, London, 1923.

Lane, R.: *Images from the Floating World*, Oxford, 1978.

Lane, R.: *Studies in Edo Literature and Art*, Tokyo and Cologne, 1978.

Michener, J.A. and Lane, R.: *Japanese Prints – from the early Masters to the Modern*, Tokyo, 1959.

Narazaki, M.: *The Japanese Print: Its Evolution and Essence*, Tokyo and Palo Alto, Cal., 1966.

Neuer, R. and Yoshida, S.: *Ukiyo-e, 250 Years of Japanese Art*, New York, 1980.

O'Neill, P.G.: *Japanese Names*, New York and Tokyo, 1972.

Roberts, L.P.: *A Dictionary of Japanese Artists*, Tokyo and New York, 1976.

Stewart, B.: *Subjects Portrayed in Japanese Colour Prints*, London, 1922.

Takahashi, S.: *Traditional Wood-block Prints of Japan*, New York, 1972.

Turk, F.A.: *The Prints of Japan*, London, 1966.

Specialist Publications:

Brandt, K.J.: *Hosoda Eishi*, Stuttgart, 1977.

Dailey, M.C. and M.A.: *The Raymond A. Bidwell Collection of Prints by Utagawa Kuniyoshi*, Springfield, Mass., 1968.

Egenolf, H.: *Tsukioka Yoshitoshi*, 1977.

Evans, T. and M.: *Shunga: The Art of Love in Japan*, London, 1975.

French, C.L.: *Shiba Kokan: Artist, Innovator, and Pioneer in the Westernization of Japan*, New York and Tokyo, 1974.

Halford, A.S. and G.M.: *The Kabuki Handbook*, Rutland, U.S.A. and Tokyo, 1956.

Hillier, J.: *Hokusai*, London, 1955.

Hillier, J.: *Utamaro*, London, 1961.

Hillier, J.: *Suzuki Harunobu*, Philadelphia, 1970.

Hillier, J.: *The Uninhibited Brush: Japanese Art in the Shijo Style*, London, 1974.

Hillier, J.: *The Art of Hokusai in Book Illustration*, London, 1980.

Illing, R.: *Japanese Erotic Art and the Life of the Courtesan*, London, 1978.

Kawakita, M.: *Contemporary Japanese Prints*, Tokyo and Palo Alto, Cal., 1967.

Keyes, R.S. and Mizushima Keiko: *The Theatrical World of Osaka Prints*, Philadelphia, 1973.

Kronhausen, E. and P.: *Erotic Art, Series I/II*, New York and London, 1968, 1970.

Lane, R.: 'The Shunga in Japanese Art' in Rawson, P. (ed.) *Erotic Art of the East*, New York and London, 1968.

Lane, R.: *Hokusai and Hiroshige*, Tokyo, 1976.

Mody, N.H.: *A Collection of Nagasaki Colour Prints and Paintings*, London and Kobe, 1939.

Meissner, K.: *Surimono*, London.

Michener, J.A.: *The Modern Japanese Print: An Appreciation*, Tokyo, 1968.

Mitchell, C.H.: *The Illustrated Books of the Nanga, Maruyama, Shijo, and other related Schools of Japan: A Bibliography*, Los Angeles, 1972.

Robinson, B.W.: *Kuniyoshi*, London, 1961.

Schamoni, W. *et al:* *Yoshitoshi*, Cologne, 1971.

Tamba, T.: *The Art of Hiroshige*, Tokyo, 1963.

Tamba, T.: *Reflections of the Culture of Yokohama in the Days of the Port Opening*, (in Japanese), Tokyo, 1972.

Waterhouse, D.B.: *Harunobu and his Age*, London, 1964.

Waterhouse, D.B.: *Images of Eighteenth Century Japan*, Toronto, 1975.

Acknowledgements and List of Illustrations

The author would like to express his gratitude to the many experts, both professional and otherwise, who have helped to make the study of Japanese art such a pleasant endeavour. In particular he wishes to thank Jack Hillier and Basil Robinson who have always been ready with helpful and friendly advice.

The author and John Calmann & Cooper Limited would like to thank the museums, galleries and collectors who allowed works from their collections to be reproduced in this book. They would also like to thank the Zauho Press for providing photographs of prints in the collection of the Tokyo National Museum.

82. Kiyomine, *Preparing to send a letter*, London, British Museum. Reproduced by courtesy of the Trustees of the British Museum
83. Shunsen (Kashosai), *New Year in the Yoshiwara*, Private Collection
84. Utamaro, *The hour of the cock*, London, British Museum. Reproduced by courtesy of the Trustees of the British Museum
85. Kikumaru, *The courtesan Ainare preparing for the tea-ceremony*, London, Victoria and Albert Museum
86. Eizan, *The courtesan Misado of the Tama-ya (House of the Jewel)*, Private Collection
87. Toyokuni III (Kunisada), *Girl amid autumn leaves*, Private Collection
88. Kunimasa, *A geisha restringing her samisen*, Tokyo National Museum
89. Eisen, *Two contemporary beauties*, London, Victoria and Albert Museum
90. Yoshitoshi, *Courtesan of the Kaei period*, Tokyo National Museum
91. Kunisada, *Fashionable beauty with silk-winding machine*, Private Collection
92. Kuniyasu, *Girl with samisen*, London, Victoria and Albert Museum
93. Kuniyoshi, *Fuji on a fine day*, London, Victoria and Albert Museum
94. Toyokuni II (Toyoshige), *Improving weather at Enoshima*, London, Victoria and Albert Museum
95. Hiroshige, *Fuji from Satta Point*, Tokyo National Museum
96. Hokusai, *Fuji seen from Nakahara*, London, Victoria and Albert Museum
97. Hokusai, *Mirror-stand Fuji*, Private Collection
98. Hokusai, *Fuji from Ushibori*, Tokyo National Museum
99. Hokusai, *The 'Hanging-cloud' bridge at Mount Gyodo*, London, Victoria and Albert Museum
100. Hokusai, *The 'Falling Mist' waterfall*, Kansas City, Nelson Gallery – Atkins Museum (Nelson Fund)
101. Hiroshige, *Drum bridge and Setting Sun Hill at Meguro*, Roger Nyle Parisious Collection
102. Toyohiro, *Fishing boats returning to Tsukuda*, Tokyo National Museum
103. Hiroshige, *The 'throwing away the brush' peak at Sakanoshita*, Tokyo National Museum
104. Hokkei, *European ship firing a salute*, London, Victoria and Albert Museum
105. Hiroshige, *Sailing boats at Arai*, Private Collection
106. Hiroshige, *Travellers in the snow at Oi*, London, Victoria and Albert Museum
107. Eisen, *Returning boats at Shibaura*, Cambridge, Fitzwilliam Museum. Reproduced by permission of the Syndics of the Fitzwilliam Museum
108. Kunitora, *Sunrise at Futami*, Private Collection
109. Hiroshige II, *The harbour of Muronotsu, Harima Province, in snow*, Private Collection
110. Koryusai, *Crane and Bamboo*, Chicago, Art Institute of Chicago
111. Taki Katei, *Bamboos*, Private Collection
112. Shumman, *Owl on magnolia branch*, London, Victoria and Albert Museum
113. Shigenaga, *Silver pheasants and waterfall*, University of Manchester, Whitworth Art Gallery
114. Koryusai, *Chrysanthemums*, Chicago, Art Institute of Chicago
115. Hokusai, *Two cranes on a snowy pine*, Minneapolis, Minneapolis Institute of Art (Gale Collection)
116. Hokusai, *Tiger lilies*, Tokyo National Museum
117. Hokusai, *Kingfisher, iris and pinks*, London, Victoria and Albert Museum
118. Hiroshige, *Kingfisher and hydrangea*, Tokyo National Museum
119. Hiroshige, *Peacock on aronia branch*, Tokyo National Museum
120. Kyosai, *Two crows on a flowering plum in winter*, Private Collection
121. Eisen, *Bamboo and moon*, University of Manchester, Whitworth Art Gallery
122. Kuniyoshi, *Shimamura Danjo Takanori*, Private Collection
123. Yoshitoshi, *Hotei and the moon of enlightenment*, Private Collection
124. Toyokuni III (Kunisada), *Self portrait of the artist*, Private Collection
125. Hokuju, *Monkey Bridge in Koshu Province*, London, Victoria and Albert Museum
126. Kuniyoshi, *Sosan returning to his mother*, Private Collection
127. Utamaro, *Rice locust, red dragon-fly, pinks and chinese bell flowers*, London, British Museum. Reproduced by courtesy of the Trustees of the British Museum
128. Kiyomasu, *Shoki the demon queller*, Chicago, Art Institute of Chicago
129. Shunei, *Asahina attempting to restrain Soga no Goro*, University of Manchester, Whitworth Art Gallery
130. Kuniyoshi, *Nozarashi Satosuke*, Private Collection
131. Eisen, *Sparrows and camellia*, London, Victoria and Albert Museum
132. Nangaku, *Ripe persimmons*, London, Victoria and Albert Museum
133. Kiyochika, *The village headman Sogoro pleading with the old ferryman*, Private Collection
134. Yoshitoshi, *The actor Bando Hikosaburo V as Kagekiyo*, Private Collection
135. Kunisada, *The actor Matsumoto Koshiro V as Nikki Danjo*, Private Collection
136. Kitao Masayoshi, *Warbler and peonies*, London, British Museum. Reproduced by courtesy of the Trustees of the British Museum
137. Kuniyoshi, *Oniwaka-maru fighting a giant carp*, Private Collection
138. Toyokuni III (Kunisada), *The actor Bando Hikosaburo V as the ghost of O-Iwa*, Private Collection
139. Toyokuni III (Kunisada), *The ghost of Yasukata*, Private Collection
140. Hokusai, *Ghost of Kohada Koheiji*, Tokyo National Museum
141. Kuniyoshi, *The actor Nakamura Utaemon IV as the ghost of Otaka Shuzen*, Private Collection
142. Kunisada, *The warrior-monk Yokogawa Kakuhan*, Private Collection
143. Kuniyoshi, *Tammeijiro Genshogo slaying Orin*, Private Collection
144. Harunobu, *Young woman in a sudden shower*, Chicago, Art Institute of Chicago
145. Kunisada, *Hangaku defending the gate*, Private Collection
146. Hokusai, *Autumn maple leaves on Tsutaya River*, London, British Museum. Reproduced by courtesy of the Trustees of the British Museum
147. Kuniyoshi, *Yoko and the tiger*, Private Collection
148. Shumman, *White and pink peonies with purple iris*, London, Victoria and Albert Museum
149. Hokusai, *Crow, sword and plum blossom*, Tokyo National Museum
150. Sadahide, *A dragon and two tigers*, London, Victoria and Albert Museum
151. Yoshimori, *Nichiren calming the storm with an invocation*, London, Victoria and Albert Museum
152. Sadahiro, *Chasing fire-flies*, Private Collection
153. Shunko, *The actor Iwai Hanshiro IV*, University of Manchester, Whitworth Art Gallery
154. Shunsho, *The actor Nakamura Nakazo II*, Tokyo National Museum
155. Koryusai, *The courtesan Hanaogi (Flower-fan) of the House of the Fan, with an attendant*, Chicago, Art Institute of Chicago
156. Toyokuni, *The actor Segawa Kikunojo III*, Private Collection
157. Kuniyoshi, *Girl washing a patterned cloth*, Private Collection
158. Kuniyoshi, *Girl in a boat by night*, Private Collection
159. Hiroshige, *The Naruto rapids in Awa Province*, London, Victoria and Albert Museum
160. Gakutei, *Court poetess at a writing table*, London, Victoria and Albert Museum
161. Kunisada, *The actor Nakamura Shikan II*, Tokyo National Museum
162. Anonymous, *Fashionable song – 'No harmony'*, Private Collection
163. Hokkei, *Shoki encouraging a small demon to show off his tricks*, London, Victoria and Albert Museum
164. Ashiyuki, *The actor Arashi Rikan II as Mashiba Hisayoshi (Hideyoshi)*, Private Collection
165. Hokushu, *Actor Nakamura Utaemon III as Ishikawa Goemon*, Philadelphia, Philadelphia Museum of Art
166. Nagasaki-e (anon.), *Foreign steamships*, Private Collection
167. Yoshitora, *A port in the United States*, London, Victoria and Albert Museum
168. Hirosada, *The actor Nakamura Utaemon IV as Higuchi no Jiro*, Courtesy of Robin Kennedy
169. Shigeharu, *The actor Sawamura Kunitaro II*, Private Collection
170. Hirosada, *The actors Ichikawa Ebizo V as Nippon Daemon and Okawa Hashizo as Nakasaina*, Private Collection
171. Shigemasa, *Dutchmen and elephant*, Private Collection
172. J. vander Schley, *Map of Nagasaki*, Private Collection
173. Chinnen, *Young woman threading a needle*, Private Collection
174. Hasui, *Snow at Mukaijima*, Private Collection
175. Nagasaki-e (anon.), *Dutch horseman*, London, British Museum. Reproduced by courtesy of the Trustees of the British Museum
176. Nagasaki-e (anon.), *Dutch man and woman*, London, British Museum. Reproduced by courtesy of the Trustees of the British Museum
177. Yoshikazu, Detail from *The interior of an American Ship*, Private Collection
178. Shinsui, *Girl washing linen*, London, British Museum. Reproduced by courtesy of the Trustees of the British Museum
179. Shoun, *Winter scene*, Private Collection
180. Kunitoshi, *The new railway station*, Private Collection
181. Goshun and Yacho, *Festival dancers*, London, Victoria and Albert Museum
182. Chinnen, *The gardener*, Private Collection
183. Shoson (Koson), *Heron in the snow*, Private Collection
184. Zeshin, *Crows in flight*, Private Collection
185. Goyo, *The model Tomi in a blue, floral robe combing her hair*, London, British Museum. Reproduced by courtesy of the Trustees of the British Museum
186. Shinsui, *Girl with fan*, London, British Museum. Reproduced by courtesy of the Trustees of the British Museum
187. Natori Shunsen, *The actor Ichikawa Ennosuke II*, London, British Museum. Reproduced by courtesy of the Trustees of the British Museum
188. Koitsu, *Lake Kawaguchi at the foot of Mount Fuji*, Private Collection
189. Elizabeth Keith, *Oriental Market*, Private Collection
190. Urushibara, *Tulips in a vase*, Private Collection
191. Sekino, *Night in Montmartre*, Dr and Mrs James B. Austin Collection

174

Index